Free Whe

or

Tony's Bicycle Book

Anthony E Thorogood

© Copyright Anthony E Thorogood 2015/2025

Contents

Intro   9

The Brand New All Singing & Dancing Retro Bicycle
A Guv'nor on Television

Part One   12
The Invention of the Bicycle
To Begin at the Beginning
The Draisine
Freewheel
The Penny Farthing
The Rover
Brooks Saddle
Dunlop's Pneumatic Tyres
Reynolds Tubing Company
Sturmey Archer Hub Gears
Derailleur
The Parabike
Lycra 1958
Carbon Fibre Reinforced Polymer
The Mountain Bike
The Fixie

The Future

Part Two   39
Bicycle Companies
The Raleigh Bicycle Company
Cairo Cappers
The Flying Pigeon
Hero and Atlas
Handcrafted
Designer

Part Three   57
Bicycles I have Known
To School on a Super Elliot
Around Adelaide on a Crannaford
A Revell in London
On Tour to Oxford
An Abandoned Relic in Yorkshire
Riccardo to Belair
A Mountain Bike to Nowhere
The Back Streets of Burra on a Linus Gaston 3

Part Four   73
Books on Bicycles
The Wheels of Chance
Three Men on the Bummel

Richard's Bicycle Book
Bike Snob
Just Ride
The Bicycle Owners Handbook
Cycle Chic

Part Five 80
Boys on Bikes
Mulga Bill's Bicycle
Left for Dead
The Skegness Wheelers Cycling Club
A Hercules Racer
A Malvern Star Dragster
Basingstoke's Sleeping Beauty

Part Six 94
Girls on Wheels
The Early Days
The Step Through
Emancipation
How I Learnt to Ride a Bicycle
Daisy
Sensible Dress
Mapp and Lucia
Dinah's Engagement Ring
Near Miss

Tangled in the Brambles
Samantha a 26 inch Red Step Through
Jane's Semi-Racer
Swinging London
Dressed to Kill
The Pushbike Song
A Snake in the Grass
Love on Two Wheels
Tripping
Lightweight Frames
Ros's Grand Tour of Holland

Part Seven   120
A Bicycle Ride Through Southern England
Part One: London to Ramsgate and Back
Part Two: Swanage Here I Come
Part Three: Swanage to Land's End and Back

Freewheeling Extended 2025

Part Eight   141
Long Distance
Crossing the Nullarbor
A Bicycle Made for Five

Training and Racing Bicycles
LEJOG & JOGLE
Highland Fling
The Way of the Roses
The Katy Trail
Hell on Earth

Part Nine   168
Collecting
The Weird and the Wonderful

Part Ten   173
Short & Sweet
In the Bag
In the Drink
In the Flesh
In the Wind
There is a tide in the affairs of Man
A Hero of our Time
Boots an' All
Freedom

Part Eleven   181
Cycling Down Under
The Bay of Fires on a Linus Gaston 3

Speed Five
Guv'nor
The Oatlands Rail Trail
The Scottsdale Rail Trail
The Blue Mountains Rail Trail
The Yarra Valley Rail Trail
The Wine Connoisseurs Rail Trail

My philosophy of life: 2025

If a person is riding a bike they must be a good person!
Happy Riding!
Anthony Thorogood

Intro
The All New All Singing and Dancing Retro Bicycle

A Guv'nor on Television

I was watching television, I don't do it often but I did, and there on the little screen, we only have a small television I hate those ugly newfangled big screens, was a Pashley Guv'nor, a retro bike harking back to... well the 1930's, it had clean lines, looked like a classic bicycle, was beautifully put together and looked a real gem. I love bicycles but I hate the modern carbon fibre road bikes. Now real bikes are back with beautiful clean lines and a classic bicycle shape and I have come in from the cold.

The Pashley Guv'nor and the Pashley Speed 5 are modelled on the old track bikes of the 1930's. Girls' bikes are back too with their upright sitting position, curved main frame, comfortable snub nosed seats (so they can wear a dress) and those swing back handlebars designed to be held easily. Girls' bikes come in a beautiful range of vibrant colours and have a basket, the basket is back. I must admit I have always been prejudice against girls' bikes because they can have a bit of a wobble, the frame not being quite as strong and they tend to be a bit heavier, but my wife, Sue, has a Linus mixte, she fell in love with the rosewood colour and the feel of the bike and I can tell you as a fact it looks good and it is light and handles beautifully. Girls' bikes now have a great feel, so do girls but I won't go into that here as I don't want to be labelled a sexist.

Not only is the classic bike in but stylish dressing on one's deadly treadly is back. Take a look at the book and the blog *Cycle Chic* by Mikael Colville-Andersen, his manifesto states: one's bike should not cost more than the clothes the rider is wearing, the bike must have a stand, a bell, a chain guard, mudguards and a basket, the rider must choose style over speed and no lycra. The websites for companies like Brooks, the saddle people, Pashley, one of the leaders in retro bikes, and Linus, a Californian bike maker, all show bikes being ridden by stylishly dressed people with panache rather than badly dressed people in racing lycra. Grant Petersen of the book *Just Ride* fame has a different take on the modern bike, he also rejects lycra and carbon fibre racing bikes, he designs very good looking machines but he believes a bike is a workhorse for everyday use, and especially overnight camping trips, and his company sell some of the best looking and most useful saddle bags available in the marketplace.

For both men and women there are a range of classic bikes available today, some based on the safety bike, the first real bicycle, and then there are a series based on the Cafe Racer (pronounced caff racer) of the Ton-Up Boys from England in the 1950's and 1960's. They had stripped back motor bikes with short handlebars adapted for a quick fun race and the bicycle boys have now adapted this concept and styling to create the Cafe Racer with inverted North Road handlebars, classic slack geometry, (what the hell is that you may say, we will get into that later, I'm really not sure what it means myself but what a brilliant phrase) and, getting back to the bikes, the stripped back styling with steel or chromology frames to create a sensational looking classic bicycle.

Part One
The Invention of the Bicycle

To Begin at the Beginning

The beginning is always a good place to start even if the beginning is the end. Bikes started in Germany with a funny old doctor, no not a doctor, a funny old Baron, who wanted to design a mechanical horse! Why bother about the history, get on with it you say. Well I am a historian, that is I went to Adelaide University and studied law, so how does that make me a historian? I hated law, I failed law and so moved back to my old love history and studied history for 4 years, I even got an honours degree in it. Getting back to bicycles, I believe to love someone, or something, properly and this book is about loving your bike, you have to know something about it, it's like when you get a new girlfriend or boyfriend, as the case may be, you want to know something of their history and about how they got to be where they are today, the same with the bike. Anyway Baron Draisine invented the bicycle in 1817.

So on to bikes. As thousands of horses died from crop failure, no feed, Baron Draisine invented what he called The Running Machine. It had two iron shod wheels, was made of wood, had a rear brake and you could steer it but you propelled it by pushing it along with your feet, not much good for a twenty mile hike and it would play havoc with ladies stilettos. Draisine saw the need and invented the solution, on its maiden voyage it did thirteen kilometres in less than an hour.

The Draisine 1817
Bikes have been around for two hundred years, in 2017 it will be their 200th birthday. The first bike, the Draisine, was a two wheeled wooden vehicle designed in Germany but the first use of the word bicycle was in France in the 1860's. There are claims that a student of Leonardo da Vinci designed the first treadly in 1493 and, not wanting to be outdone by the Germans or the Italians, there is also a claim that the French designed the first peddlo in1791. Be that as it may, I think the Draisine is the front runner in the first bike stakes. As with all important inventions the bicycle evolved. Ideas were tossed about and slowly the modern bicycle emerged, it is the result of the collective thought of humanity rather than one brilliant man or woman.

The first commercial bike was the Draisine and it was manufactured in commercial numbers in both Germany and France, it was also called a velocipede and even a hobby-horse. The bicycle is basically a horse with wheels. I read somewhere that the bicycle was a development of the wheelbarrow, I would love to see the person who came up with that idea peddle a wheelbarrow for thirteen kilometres!

An English improved version, popularly called the hobby-horse, was introduced in 1819 and was a hit in London society. But riders on the pavement were fined and accidents occurred and the craze for the velocipede, hobby horse and the Draisine died a death. However the phoenix rose from the ashes. In France cranks were added and pedals mounted on the front wheels and a metal frame was used and the modern bicycle was born. A company was formed just for the manufacture of the new machines, Michaux et Cie, and the bicycle craze took off again.

In England these early bicycles made of iron, with iron wheels were christened boneshakers, you can easily imagine what such a machine was like to ride over the cobbled streets of the time. The bicycle was a commercial success but had its problems, stability wasn't good, comfort was poor and steering worse, try steering a front wheel with peddles on it whilst peddling! These problems, or the solution to these problems, eventually led to the development of what we call today the penny farthing.

Two things which improved the bicycle were ball bearings and solid rubber tyres and with these the bicycle became a social hit with special rinks developed where people went to ride the newfangled contraptions. However once the craze had run its course the popularity of these bikes waned. You still see it today, bicycle design goes through crazes, we have had the carbon fibre road bike and now the mountain bike seems to control the streets of cities as well as the sides of mountains and now there is a craze for retros (old 60's and 70's style bikes) and fixies, old style racing bikes with a fixed wheel, no gears and dressed in bright luminous colours.

Freewheel 1869
To cycle up a hill can be darn hard work but one of the greatest pleasures in life is to freewheel down the other side. Sue, my wife, compares it to flying, like a bird not in an aeroplane. Apparently the freewheel, that is the ability of a bike to move

forward without its pedals going round, as do fixed wheel bikes or fixies, was first invented in 1869 by a chap named William Van Anden (he sounds as if he could be Dutch) he seems to have put some sort of ratchet device in the hub of the front wheel, we are talking here about the boneshakers that were peddled directly from the front wheel.

The first popular freewheel bike was the whippet manufactured by Messrs Linley, Biggs and Archer from 1889. The whippet had an expanding chain wheel two speed gear, to change gears one had to back pedal so it needed a free wheel. This bike needed a good brake and had one that was applied to the rim of the back wheel by the left foot, it sounds a bit dubious but when I went to school some boys rode bikes without brakes and used their feet, well their shoes, applied to the back wheel to stop! The whippet actually looked like an expensive modern mountain bike so really nothing is new.

The Penny Farthing 1870's
Then came the penny farthing, the high wheel bicycle or the ordinary which was developed in Victorian England and was especially popular there. Basically the penny farthing was a bicycle with pedals on the huge front wheel, one sat on the front

wheel, metaphorically speaking, if one literally sat on the front wheel it would play havoc with one's ability to reproduce the species, and the rear wheel was very small hence the term penny farthing, a penny was a big English coin and a farthing a small English coin worth a quarter of a penny and about a quarter of the size. The advantage of this arrangement, the big and small wheel, was that the machine was geared up to go faster and on rough terrain the penny farthing was a smoother ride than the old boneshaker as the big wheel went over bumps with ease, the disadvantage was that if you stopped quickly, or hit a bad bump in the road, over you went, this was called coming a cropper or taking a header. Broken wrists were common and riders were even killed in falls.

Apparently it was a Frenchman who invented the penny farthing but the English manufacturers who made it popular. As well as the development of the penny farthing in the 1870's, ball bearings, solid rubber tyres and hollow steel frames became the thing and the bicycle industry started to take off. American companies began manufacturing these bikes and formulated all sorts of modern adaptions to the production process including mass production. They supported improved roads and advertised aggressively bringing a spurt of popularity to the bicycle in the USA.

However cycling was still the sport of energetic rich young men. HG Wells in his book *The Wheels of Change* describes a workman on a penny farthing: *a workman riding to destruction on a very tall ordinary*, so the ordinary was also used by the working class, this was perhaps when they had been discarded by the rich who moved on to safety bikes and the poor could snap up a penny farthing cheaply. The description of the ordinary as very tall points to one of the reasons why they were expensive rich men's toys, each bike was customised to the length of the rider's leg, the size of the front wheel was directly proportional to the owners legs so mass production was not possible.

The Rover 1885
Next came the safety bicycle which became a means of transport for people in all walks of life, in fact the safety bicycle helped liberate not only the common working man but also women from all social classes. The most famous safety bicycle, the Rover, was developed in 1885 by John Kemp Starley in Coventry England. The Rover had two wheels of the same size, a chain drive to the back wheel and a

triangular diamond frame and was the first bicycle that could be instantly recognised as the father of the modern bike. It was said at the time that the Rover *set the pattern for the world.* Not only was the safety bicycle invented at this time but Dunlop pneumatic tyres appeared in 1888 giving a much smoother ride for the safety bicycle and the new diamond frame design was much more efficient and stronger. Another famous safety bike was the whippet, already mentioned, it was patented in 1885, it had sprung suspension and even a derailleur with a magnificent selection of two gears!

In HG Wells's books the words diamond frame, safety bicycle and Dunlop figure highly when he describes a bicycle, this shows the significance of these developments in the collective brain of the time. What's more the safety bicycle was now cheaper to manufacture than the penny farthing and ordinary people could afford at least a second hand bike.

Brooks Saddle 1882
The saddle is one of the most important parts of a bike and can give you a hard uncomfortable ride. I'm no expert on saddles but in my cycling life I have had 3 bikes with Brooks B17 saddles and for

my current bike I have an el cheapo vinyl covered padded plastic thing, it actually looks good, not as good as a Brooks though, and it is fairly comfortable. My wife insisted on a padded sprung seat of the female variety with a snub nose and she finds it comfortable so she is happy to cycle.

One book I dipped into suggested the best seat was made in Italy by a company called Cippeli, or something like that, but Brooks have a very high reputation and are certainly some of the most elegant looking saddles that you can put on a bike. Brooks was established in 1866 by a gent called John Boultbee Brooks. Should have called his saddles Boultbee:

'What are you riding?'

'A Boultbee.'

'Cool!'

He started the company in Birmingham and was into horse harnesses, saddles for horses and that sort of thing and in 1878 old Brooks's horse carked it so he loaned a cycle and was the ride ever uncomfortable. He decided he could make a better bike saddle, no worries, and his first bike saddle was patented in1882 and was a great success. As well as saddles Brooks made bags and accessories for bikes and motorbikes but business is not always straight forward and the Brooks Saddle Company was taken over by Raleigh Bicycle Company in 1962 since then there has been a management buyout, I think, and even a takeover by an Italian firm if my memory serves me rightly.

Some of the old advert's for Brooks saddles are interesting:

1921: *We believe, and are convinced that all riders will agree, that a comfortable saddle is one of the greatest, if not the greatest asset to real pleasure cycling.* I would agree with that.

1926: *The wise man who is taking up cycling in any form, or changing his style of riding, due either to age or inclination, will exercise great care in the selection of his saddle.* I'd agree with that too.

So what makes a leather saddle so good, well the story goes that after many hours of riding the saddle slowly moulds to the shape of your body. I have been looking at Brooks saddles myself and fancy one of the sprung B17's however the biggest drawback with a leather saddle is that you can't get it wet.

In Richard's Bicycle Book there is a good story about saddles: *Two of my friends set off from London to India on their bikes, and within two days were each swearing a blue streak at their saddles – one a leather Brooks and the other a Stella Italia foam filled anatomic. Discomfort mounted and when raging pain bought the duo to a halt a few days later, as a last resort they switched saddles. Suddenly all was bliss and they completed the rest of the 6,000 mile journey without complaint.*

Dunlop's Pneumatic Tyre 1887
A Scotsman in Ireland invented the pneumatic tyre and what a great breakthrough that was. It really saves on a sore bum and boneshaker joints. The Scotsman's name was John Boyd Dunlop, he was a vet, and one day he watched his son on a tricycle with solid rubber tyres going round and round over cobbles, it was a slow and bumpy ride and gave his son headaches so Dunlop wrapped the wheels of the trike in rubber sheets, glued them together and inflated them with a football pump, thus Dunlop developed the first air cushioned tyres. And a little known cycle racer, using Dunlop's new invention, won seven out of eight bicycle races within a year of Dunlop's invention. To commercialise these new tyres the Pneumatic Tyre and Booth's Cycle Agency

Co Ltd was formed in 1889 and, as they say, the rest is history.

Reynolds Tubing Company 1897

John Reynolds founded Reynolds Tubing Company in Birmingham England in 1889. It was a development of a much earlier company that made nails. In 1897 the company created the process for making steel tubes which were thicker at the ends and this created light strong tubes. The double butted tube 531 was created in 1934 and, before the development of modern strange materials for lightweight bike frames, Reynolds were number one in the market place for light weight frames. Of late Reynolds have developed new tubing for bicycles such as their 953 using steel with extremely thin walls but still very strong and light.

When I was a boy the bike to own was made of Reynolds 531, had a Brooks saddle and Campagnolo fittings. Alas I never had the money for that!

Sturmey Archer Hub Gears 1902

Sturmey Archer originated in Nottingham England in 1902 and specialised in the 3 speed hub gear released in 1936. The company was set up by Henry Sturmey and James Archer under the umbrella of the Raleigh Bicycle Company also of Nottingham. The gears are said to be elliptical or planetary, I guess that means that they go round in circles, and they have different sized cogs that move the bike at varying speeds. I know there is also a five speed hub in production which is fitted to the Pashley Speed 5.

Compared to the derailleur Sturmey Archer are not perhaps so all singing and dancing but my God they are easy to use, need very little maintenance and look much more beautiful than the ugly derailleur does. The truth about the derailleur is that of all the people who have them, 95% in a recent survey, don't know how to use them and just stick in one gear. The opposite applies to the Sturmey Archer 3 speed, most people, 95% according to a recent survey, who have them use the gears all the time! I have used both types of gears and I enjoy a Sturmey Archer for its ease of use and I would now love to try a Sturmey Archer 5 speed.

Derailleur 1885
In this book I have been rubbishing the derailleur gear system however in my life I have owned four bikes with derailleurs and I did very well with three of them, there wasn't a hill I couldn't climb. I had a 10 speed derailleur on three of the bikes which was

great but on the fourth bike there were God knows how many gears and it was awful. Nowadays you get something like a 30 speed derailleur, that's derailleurs gone mad! I rode one of these 30 speed bikes and hated it, enough said, I am sure someone loves them! My main contention is that your average cyclist, even those who think they are Lance Armstrong, don't know how to use their derailleur and usually start the ride in a fairly low gear and end the ride without having changed gear at all. Gears should be easy to use and help a cyclist not hinder them. Many cyclists are scared of their gears, for God's sake get a bike with a 3 speed Sturmey Archer with a hand grip to change the gears. My wife has one and she loves it, she not only loves it but she uses her gears very well, she uses them when heading into the wind and to help on hill climbs, when she had a derailleur she would stop, get off and I would stop, get on her bike and change her gears for her, most people don't even do that.

The word derailleur by the way, is French and it means that a train has come off the tracks and is derailed. Compared to the internal hub gears the derailleur is basically cave man technology, however, not another bloody however, it is highly developed cave man technology. Derailleurs are a variable-ratio transmission system and basically give the chain a shove from one sprocket to another and there are lots of sprockets. So you have a nob near the handlebars that pulls the shifter by a series of cables and then the chain is derailed onto another sprocket, simple.

The whippet bicycle designed in England in 1885 had a two cog derailleur and there were others built at the time. The Frenchman Paul de Vivie invented a two speed derailleur in 1905, other systems were introduced and in 1937 the derailleur was allowed in the Tour de France, (called by one writer: That Boring Old Race Around France) apparently before this, in the Tour de France, to change gears one had to stop and change wheels!

In 1949 Campagnolo, an Italian bicycle maker, introduced the Gran Sport and in 1964 Suntour invented the slant-parallelogram rear derailleur that had easier shifting and then the derailleur took off. I remember around the early seventies suddenly the general cycling public discovered the derailleur and the ten speed bike became the bike you had to have. Sturmey Archer hub gears, no gear and fixed wheel bikes started to disappear and a bike had to have ten speeds, dropped racing handlebars, toe clips and no mud guards and 27 x 1¼ inch tyres (racing style) the craze for look-alike racing bikes had begun. So the modern derailleur is brilliant, perhaps, if you know how to use it but most people are bewildered by it even those cyclists who pretend to be all singing and dancing.

The Parabike 1942
In World War Two the British army commissioned BSA, Birmingham Small Arms Company, a manufacturer of rifles and bicycles as well as motor bikes, to produce a lightweight folding bicycle to be dropped out of aeroplanes with the paratroopers to increase their mobility. BSA's design was successful and over 70,000 Parabikes were produced. The bike had folding handlebars, seat and pedals, and had an elliptical frame, that means curved, for strength, they came in green, and also brown when the green paint ran out, and the paratrooper would jump out of the plane with the folded bike held to his chest. Bloody hell it would be bad enough jumping out of a plane but jumping out of a plane with a bicycle strapped to your chest, wouldn't get me doing that! The bike was so designed that the seat and handlebars hit the ground

first in order to protect the wheels from buckling, but what about the poor bloody paratrooper?

Originally called the Airborne Bike, after the war christened the Parabike, it was first used in a highly successful raid on a German radar station near the French coast, the Paras were dropped inland away from the radar station so as not to alert the garrison and then they rode their bikes to the radar station, captured it, dismantled the radar, shot their way to the beach and were picked up by landing craft. The point of the raid was to capture and study the German radar of the time and the raid was one hundred per cent successful.

The Parabike was used by the second wave of infantry landing on D Day as they moved inland, the bikes were then discarded much to the joy of the French peasants who were seen riding around on Parabikes after the landings. The Parabike was also used at the battle of Arnhem where British Paras captured a critical bridge only to be defeated by German tanks, the Parabike proved no match for a German Tiger Tank with its 88mm gun and thick armour. British tankies also used Parabikes as run abouts hitching them to the back of their tanks. After the war the Airborne Bike, as it was still called, was released commercially by BSA as they changed from war production to civilian production and in their adverts they called the machines Parabikes.

Bicycles were used extensively by the German army later in World War Two as they were unable to use trains or trucks to move their troops as the allied air forces targeted and destroyed them. The Germans moved troops by bike at night in both Europe and Russia. In Russia it was hard work because of the rough roads. I read a story of two young German recruits cycling for a month to get to the front and then being captured by British paratroopers before they had fired a shot, lucky them really. The Japanese Army used bicycle troops in their spectacularly successful conquest of Malaysia and Singapore. Was that 1942? It seems it was the speed and mobility of the bike troops that won the day.

Lycra 1958
So we are getting to recent times now. We have invented the two wheeled horse, turned it into a penny farthing, improved that and released the safety bicycle, got pneumatic tyres, relatively comfortable seats, gears, lightweight frames and

suddenly we get lycra, all that brilliant innovation ends up with lycra sitting on it. I ask you?

Lycra, love it or hate it, is with us and many cyclists love it. It is the image, young and old men and even women dream about racing in the Tour de France and they buy expensive carbon fibre bikes and lycra racing gear and every Sunday morning go racing with their mates, inevitably they end up in a coffee shop drinking cappuccino and eating cake. To me lycra makes you look ugly, unless you are a young slim racing professional, and makes you perspire. The Sunday morning lycra set always look hot and sweaty. But what is this lycra stuff? Lycra has other names, spandex (expands inverted) or elastane, and is an elastic durable and strong fibre that was invented by Joseph Shivers at DuPont's Virginia USA in 1958 and was introduced into the clothing industry in 1962.

It seems to be made by a process called dry spinning and consists of five steps: First create the prepolymer by mixing a couple of ingredients with great sounding names, I think not, macroglycol and diisocyanate, don't sprinkle it on your cornflakes. Next they get into a chain extension reaction by adding diamine, it is then thinned with a solvent.

Now we get to the spinning bit, the solution is pumped into a spinning cell where it is forced through a metal plate, a spinneret which forces the solution into strands, they are then exposed to nitrogen and solvent gas and turn into solid strands. I hope you are taking all this in as I will test you later. So we are up to the forth bit of the process this is simple the solid bands are bundled together to achieve the desired thickness. Now finally the bands are treated with a finishing agent something like magnesium stearate to stop the fibres sticking together, the fibres are then transferred onto a spool.

Now I will tell you how woollen jumpers are made as I live in a wool producing region. It is all very natural and, in comparison, chemical free. Sheep are heavily into the creation of wool, sheep eat grass, they turn the grass into wool, once a year the woollen fleece is shorn off the sheep by big tough heavy drinking blokes called shearers, the wool is washed, carded and spun, and this can be done by hand if you wish, then you can knit a jumper or a beany if you are so inclined to keep your head warm.

Carbon Fibre Reinforced Polymer 1975

The first carbon fibre frame, an Exxon Graftek, came out in 1975 and flopped, it didn't reappear until the mid 1980's. It's quite a mouthful is carbon fibre reinforced polymer but what does it mean? It is a strongish, lightweight, composite material that is expensive and cracks and you don't know that it has cracked, this situation could prove fatal, and it also makes for ugly bikes. I'm still not sure exactly how it is made but it contains fibres and resins and must be put together like fibreglass where there is some sort of matting material, a couple of ingredients are mixed, brushed on and set rock hard, but don't quote me here because quite frankly I don't know and to be even more frank I don't care, I'm not a fan.

In carbon fibre the binding polymer is often a thermoset such as polyester or vinyl ester but even nylon is sometimes used. The composite can contain other fibres such as aramid or ultrahigh molecular weight polyethylene or glass fibre as well as carbon fibre. The properties of the final product are affected by the additives added to the resin, commonly silica is used but rubber or carbon nanotubes can be used – I've lost you! I've lost me!

Carbon fibre is very popular in racing bikes it is strong, light weight and can be moulded into any shape desired but it is brittle, it can't handle hard knocks, it is vulnerable to fatigue failure, it is expensive and worse still it is ugly. When all is said and done however if it is speed you want, and lightweight bikes give you a bit more speed, then carbon fibre is the bike for you, eating less doughnuts at the coffee shop after the ride would work even better.

The Mountain Bike late 70's
Yes I am totally prejudiced against mountain bikes, to me they look like kids' bikes and are not beautiful. I once helped my brother ferry a couple of good quality mountain bikes from his workshop, he was a carpenter, to his house and I was quite impressed so I bought a mountain bike but it wasn't long before I hated it. The real problem was that it was so slow, it took me forever to get anywhere, I think this was caused by small wheels and low gearing, it also wasn't beautiful, it was a bit of an ugly duckling that would never turn in to a swan, I didn't like riding it and I gave it away. So what with the carbon fibre crowd, the lycra set and the mountain bike gang I stopped riding bikes. However I read Richard's 21st Century Bicycle Book, a book

that verges a little on the dull side, but the chapter on mountain bikes came alive, Richard Ballantine loves mountain bikes.

Mountain bikes were invented by a mob of young hippy types in the late seventies and early eighties in the mountains of California. People would gather on forest roads at the top of mountains and tear downhill on their converted paper boy cruiser bikes. These early conversions sparked the mountain bike, and some great innovations in general bike design, and Richard took it up in England and promoted the new style of cycling and when it comes right down to it, at a time when the ten speed dominated bicycle design, what's wrong with inventing a new bike suited to a specific purpose, absolutely nothing. The problem today is that everyone seems to have a mountain bike and mountain bikes are not good city bikes or touring bikes and often are no good for girls who want to dress a little bit chic! Bring on the step through, the fixie and the retro.

So what is a mountain bike? It is a highly geared, up to thirty gears, strong, sometimes heavy, fat tyred 26 inch wheeled off road machine designed to take the bumps and spills of charging down a mountain. I remember in the late seventies I would ride my

Sturmey Archer semi racer (normal bike) up to Golden Grove and charge around the dirt roads there, I even found an abandoned scrambles track, called Snake Gully, and I would charge around there as well. My friend David Blight at the same time charged around the dirt tracks at a place called Brown Hill Creek and he managed to destroy several conventional bikes. Another friend of mine, Tony Statton and his mates would push their bikes up Mt Lofty, this would have to be in the late 60's, and they charged down at speeds of 45 miles an hour, one time he was charging down and he only had a foot brake and the chain came off and, terrified, he sped at an horrific rate down the hill using his new shoes as breaks. His shoes were wrecked and he got into a lot of trouble for that. The following week however he was off up the mountain again. It is probably in boys genes to charge around on bikes so the mountain bike fulfils a need, I still don't like them.

The Fixie 2014

The trendy bike nowadays is a fixed gear or fixie. Cycling has come full circle back to the old days of the safety bicycle. Gears and freewheels arrived, gears and bikes generally got more and more complex and expensive, nowadays a bike can have thirty gears, and a space age carbon fibre frame only good for five years, so there has been a reaction. It is now cool to have a simple bike not even with a freewheel. No brakes, no wires, no guards, no carrier just clean old fashioned lines and yes in spite of their luminous crazy colours, fixies look quite beautiful. One of their great advantages is that they are really quite easy to maintain, you don't have to be a nuclear scientist to work the gears, there are none. They are inexpensive, although there are expensive versions out there, they have beautiful clean lines as opposed to the chunky ugliness of the carbon fibre bikes and they can still be quite light weight.

Fixies have two real down sides, they are difficult to stop as they use the technique of peddling backwards to brake and one has to peddle downhill as well as up. Bloody hell it's bad enough peddling up hill. Also going round corners is slightly more difficult at speed. One point in their favour, they are good for doing tricks, you can actually go backwards on a fixie and they apparently have a lovely old fashioned feel of freedom and being at one with one's bike. A lot of old bike professionals rail against them which just makes them more popular with the young at heart.

Fixies aren't new, as I said earlier, and were for many years a big part of track racing, so some fixies look like old racers with dropped handlebars and muted colours. I saw a pair of these old fixies in the front window of a Launceston bike shop in Tasmania and they were extremely attractive, they had lovely lugs and name plaques, were beautifully simple in design and great colours. Everything else in the shop was a carbon fibre racer or a squat mountain bike, there was no comparison. Others fixies are built for the urban cyclist and one I saw had a luminous green frame with bright orange tyres and both wheels were quite different, the back wheel was plastic with a few large spokes and the front wheel was a wire spoked job. With fixies the individuality of the rider reigns supreme.

Fixed gear bicycles became the thing in New York in the 80's, they were a hit with bicycle couriers because they were easy to maintain simple and inexpensive and they, the couriers, looked for narrow handlebars for ease of traffic jamming and the new bike took off in cities around the world. Now fixies for boys and step throughs for girls are starting to replace the mountain bike on our streets and it is about time!

The Future

We need to keep spunky in the word bicycle. The velocipede was spunky in aristocratic France in 18 whatever, the penny farthing became the thing for with-it young rich English men to ride in the 1880's, the safety bicycle became a fashion item in the 1890's, then the roadsters became the bike of the common man. Then racing took off and derailleurs and drop handlebar bikes were the flavour of the month, not to forget cruisers and BMX bikes and small wheeled commuter bikes. The ten speed was in there somewhere, then mountain bikes tumbled along and took off and took over, then carbon fibre machines with lycra clad overweight middle aged riders descended upon the streets and now it's the retro, fixie and step through, with baskets, that are the bikes of the in-crowd. Bikes need to evolve and win new audiences continuously and then their simple but brilliant design will push-peddle them along into the distant future.

Part Two
Bicycle Companies

The Raleigh Bicycle Company 1885

The story of the Raleigh Bicycle Company is a tale of eat or be eaten. A young man arrives with a vision, takes on the world, builds a great company and then at the peak of its success the company starts to lose ground, goes under and re-emerges with the same branding but not quite the same vision. The truth is that companies must evolve or die.

The precursor to the Raleigh Bicycle Company was set up in 1885 by Richard Morriss Woodhead and Paul Eugene Louis Angois, together they established a bicycle workshop in Raleigh Street Nottingham and made safety bicycles. A businessman from the Nottingham lace industry, William Ellis, arrived with capital and the company started to expand. All three men, Woodhead, Angois and Ellis, had a background in the local lace industry so naturally they would make bicycles! The bicycle company under Ellis's direction expanded taking up an empty lace making factory and made up to three cycles a week and employed six men.

Ellis was soon bought out by a solicitor named Frank Bowden:

In the early part of 1887, while looking for a good specimen of the then new safety bicycle, I came across a Raleigh in London. Its patent changeable gear and other special features struck me as superior to all the others I had seen, and I purchased one upon which I toured extensively through France, Italy and England during 1887 and 1888. In the autumn of the latter year, happening to pass through Nottingham, and with the idea of, if possible, getting a still more up-to-date machine, I called upon Messrs. Woodhead and Angois, the originators and makers of the Raleigh ...

Bowden concluded that the company had a good future if it promoted its innovations, increased output, cut overheads and tailored its products to the individual and he bought a half share in it. Paul Angois was responsible for product design, Richard Woodhead was factory manager, William Ellis was, by this time, history and Frank Bowden was chairman and managing director and he made his vision happen.

The works consisted of three small workshops and a greenhouse but when Bowden arrived they rented a five storey former lace factory around the corner and by 1892 the company had expanded into another factory and a mill and they soon moved into a third factory and then moved into yet another mill. By 1913 Raleigh claimed to be the biggest bicycle manufacturer in the world occupying a seven and a half acre purpose built premises built in1897 and that wasn't the end of the company's expansion. By the early 1920's Raleigh led the world and manufactured up to 100,000 bikes a year, by 1938 it was producing nearly 500,000 bikes, by 1949 it was turning out 750,000 bikes, the majority for export, and 1951 saw over a million cycles produced. Unfortunately by this time England was getting prosperous, people wanted cars, and bike sales in the UK slumped. Raleigh handled the situation by absorbing competitors, this saw a slight increase in cycle production, they also created new products such as highly fashionable small wheeled commuter bikes which proved popular, and cruisers and dragsters, these products helped arrest the downward trend of bicycle sales.

As I wrote Raleigh ate up other companies after World War Two and became a very big concern, they even owned Sturmey Archer Gears, Brooks Saddles and Reynolds Steel Tubing. In the eighties however things started to change and the company went belly up. Raleigh in America were now made by an American company and production of bikes started to move to Japan and South East Asia. Buy outs and sell offs saw Brooks, Sturmey Archer and Reynolds go and Raleigh seems to have been acquired by a German Company who were then acquired by a Dutch company and production in the UK ceased and moved to Asia with final assembly in Holland.

In its time Raleigh owned or bought out the following English cycle manufacturers: Humber, Rudge-Whitworth, Triumph, Three Spires, BSA, New Hudson, Sunbeam, Phillips, Hercules, Norman, Sun and Carlton, quite a haul really. It's a jungle out there, you either eat or get eaten and in the end no one is immune as, after eating others, Raleigh was itself eaten.

After World War Two Raleigh became famous for their lightweight sports bikes using Sturmey Archer 3 and 5 speed gears and Reynolds lightweight steel tubing and that is how I think of Raleigh's bikes. Their greatest success was indirect and they didn't earn a penny from it, the Chinese Flying Pigeon, the most manufactured vehicle in the world, is a copy of a Raleigh roadster of the 1930s.

Cairo Cappers 1980's

If a history of the bicycle doesn't include a mention of the millions of bikes made and sold in India and China then it is just playing around at the edges of cycling. Bicycles are big in China and India and in fact all third world countries. I remember seeing a cyclist in Cairo, Egypt, cycling along single handed with the other hand helping to balance a great tray on his head. The tray was piled high with a pyramid of what we call Lebanese bread, unleavened bread or flat bread, anyway one loaf fell off and the cyclist cycled down the street, turned, came back, picked up the loaf and continued on his way all the time still balancing the great tray of bread on his head. And we think in the West that we are accomplished cyclists?

The Flying Pigeon 1950

The Flying Pigeon, supposedly a symbol of peace, was first built in China during the Korean War and is based on the Raleigh roadster of 1932. It looks like a real retro bike with its swept back handlebars, mud guards, sprung seat, chain guards, rear carrier, single speed and all, it could almost get into a Pashley catalogue, as could the classic Indian bike. Sensible roadsters have been, and still are, very popular in India, China and Africa.

In the People's Republic of China the Flying Pigeon, a strong, durable, light and beautiful bicycle, was sponsored as the Government's approved form of transport and China became known as the kingdom of the bicycle. In the early 1980's I got off a train in Guangzhou in China's south and tried to cross a road to the People's Hotel. The road was very very wide and I was carrying a heavy backpack, I stepped out onto the road and a wall of bicycles came at me, I ran back to the pavement for cover. It took me several attempts to get across that road and as I tried thousands of cyclists pedalled by. In those days a bicycle was regarded as one of the must haves of every citizen alongside a sewing machine and a watch.

The Flying Pigeon became the single most manufactured vehicle on the planet! And Deng Xiaoping, the post Maoist leader, described prosperity as a Flying Pigeon in every household. Three million flying pigeons were sold in 1986 and there was a waiting list several years long to get one. The typical colour was black but the fire department had red Pigeons, green was for China

Post and yellow orange and blue were used by businesses. However it is not all sunshine and roses these days as sales of the Flying Pigeon are very much in decline, new style bikes are available as are motorbikes, scooters and cars but the Flying Pigeon is still China's biggest selling bike and over half a billion of them are in use handed down within the family. Now the Flying Pigeon is looked on nostalgically as a symbol of the good old days and the logo of the Flying Pigeon has been recognised as a national treasure in China.

Hero and Atlas 1956
India is the second largest bicycle manufacturer in the world manufacturing twelve million bikes per annum, which is 9% of the world production, China makes 66% of the world's bikes. Here is an interesting statistic: A bicycle dealer in Patna, Bihar sells 10,000 bicycles a month, that's a lot of bikes.

Anyway getting down to brass tacks, the brothers Brijmohan Lall Munjal, Satyanand Munjal, Om Prakash Munjal and Dayanad Munjal set up a bicycle repair shop in Amritsar in 1944. The brothers moved to Ludhiana and started a bicycle manufacturing company in 1956. They thought that people in newly independent India needed cheap and convenient transport and in their first year they manufactured 639 bikes. By 1975 the Hero Bicycle Company was the largest manufacturer of bicycles in India and in 1986 Hero was in the Guinness Book of Records as the biggest manufacturer of bicycles in the world. Today it is said by the company's publicity that Hero Bicycles manufacture more than 18,500 bikes daily, that is a bloody lot of bikes.

The typical Hero is a black roadster with a very well sprung seat, mudguards, lights, a full chain guard and a carrier however the Hero Bike Co want to present a new image with state of the art carbon fibre racing bikes and mountain bikes with derailleur gears.

There is another big Indian bicycle manufacturing company, Atlas, who also turn out the classic roadster. Atlas was set up by a man named Shri Jankidas Kapur and he began in a back shed in 1951. That same year he expanded to a twenty five acre factory and turned out twelve thousand cycles, I take this info from the company blurb. The company's blurb also claims that in 1978 they emerged as India's largest cycle manufacturer and that they manufactured India's first racing bike in that same year.

Handcrafted

What can I say about Pashley - lovely bikes - it was on one of my rare stints of watching television that I first saw the Pashley Guv'nor with its black paint job, cream Schwalbe Delta Cruiser tyres and swept back North Road handlebars and I had to have one. Alas I didn't get one but I did get a Linus Gaston 3, a Pashley Guv'nor look alike. I will get back to that later. I read up on Pashley, it's a small firm in Stratford-upon-Avon, England which started in 1926 they make handcrafted bikes, using classic English components, Brooks saddles, Sturmey Archer gears, Reynolds 531 tubing, lugged frame joints and hub breaks, not to mention the classic slack geometry. I love them, especially the Speed 5 with its semi dropped handlebars, 5 speed Sturmey Archer gears and classic English racing green colours. Then I read up on their retro girls roadster and what old fashioned but beautiful things they are. Called Princess they are classic black with swept back handlebars, baskets, carriers, full chain guards and a net to stop the ladies dresses getting caught in the rear wheel. Here is what Pashley have to say:

Since the company was founded by William 'Rath' Pashley in 1926, we here at Pashley have been dedicated to hand-building high-quality bicycles and tricycles to meet the diverse and evolving needs of our customers. We are proud to be the longest-established British bicycle manufacturer and one of only three remaining here in the UK. Our bicycles are not only unique in their design and quality, but also in their connection to a well-established heritage of craftsmanship and innovation at our workshop in Stratford-upon-Avon.

After discovering Pashley I then came across Jaspa Bikes handmade in a back shed in Rugby England by two boys with a passion for bikes. They have a classic grey blue greenie colour and a real swept back handlebar but Jaspa actually specialise in hand making bikes to the customer's specifications. So here is what Jaspa have to say:

At Jaspa we believe that the bicycle is not only a machine of precision and balance, but it is a thing of immense beauty, of character and above all soul. Our bicycles are designed and built in the UK, using Brooks saddles and grips, Sturmey Archer cranks and 2 speed hubs and front drum brakes.

I didn't stop at Jaspa, I found a company in America, Two Beauts or a name like that, using old Raleigh frames to create state of the art modern bikes paying particular attention to the paint job, how many bikes does a man need? How many bikes can a man afford?

Then I found Rivendell Bikes in California, another handmade customised American machine with particularly beautiful lugs, 8 speed derailleurs nothing too complex but all you need. Rivendell Bikes seem to have a bias towards bikes for camping and touring and have a big S in the sensible stakes but at the same time produce lovely bikes. I quote Rivendell:

We've been bucking trends with lugged steel bicycle frames, wool cycling clothes, cotton bike luggage and leather saddles ever since 1994. In an industry that introduces revolutionary technological advances every season, we've stuck to what works and have flown the flags of safety, comfort and lasting value for over twenty years now. These things don't get old, even when technology does. Rivendell bikes are designed to be used hard and handed down for generations of riders.

All the bike companies I mentioned here produce beautiful handmade machines. One American company I found described its bikes as bikes you can hang on your mantelpiece and just look at. One thing however, all these handmade bikes, using classic parts, are also expensive.

Designer
The bikes I am looking at now, either most of their parts are made in Asia or they are completely made there but the design work is done in Australia or California and each company manages to build bikes with a distinct personality and a handful of style.

Unfortunately I ran out of money in my quest for a Pashley Guv'nor so I started looking at other bikes that were modern, beautiful and spunky, they are made in China but often use classic parts like the Sturmey Archer 3 speed. I found Papillionaire in Melbourne Australia making a range of rather nice retro bikes inspired by French Bikes of the 50's and 60's, with leather handlebar grips, leather saddles and 3 speed hubs. I was rather taken by their cafe racers and would have been happy to ride one of those bikes around the streets of Burra where I lived at the time. This is what Papillionaire have to say:

Papillionaire Bicycles is an Australian owned and operated company. Founded in 2009 by Alan Caras, he was soon joined by his sister, Nicola Caras. At Papillionaire, our aim is to integrate bike-riding seamlessly into your everyday life. Whether you're in jeans, a dress, a suit or flip-flops, riding a Papillionaire is easy, clean and fun, with each model customizable to suit your own unique style. We've worked tirelessly to create bikes that are not only chic and modern, but built to last a lifetime, bringing classic European design to the streets of Australia.

But Papillionaire isn't the only company selling good bikes, basically made in China, at a good price. I also found Lekker Bikes, also in Melbourne, these were inspired by classic Dutch bikes, their blurb states:

Taken from both Dutch cycle heritage and Australian beach culture. We care about the way you get around town every day, about that amazing feeling of freedom while riding around.

Every country has a brilliant range of bikes available from smallish bike companies, you don't have to settle for the old dull and boring mountain bikes anymore just get onto the internet and search and you can find a machine within your price range and you can help build a bicycle revolution. So looking around the internet, surfing they used to call it, I tried surfing once in the sea but fell off my board, back to bikes, I found Linus Bikes. Linus is a bicycle company designing bikes in California which are made in China, and I came across the Gaston 3, a stripped back cafe racer with white tyres, a black classic diamond frame and North Road handlebars and I fell in love. Sue, my wife, liked the look of the Linus mixte, what we used to call a hybrid, and she fell in love with a rosewood version. The following is taken from Linus's blurb:

Inspired by French bicycle design of the 50s and 60s we have created a bicycle that preserves the simple elegance and pure form of that golden era, but has all the benefits of modern comfort and reliability. LINUS is the utilitarian city bike... simple and reliable, but with a personality and style that makes you feel like you're in an old French movie... you're floating a little from the wine you drank at lunch... maybe instead of going back to the office you'll take a nap under a tree, go for a swim in the sea or drop by your lover's house...

What could be better as an image for cycling than the above!

We bought two Linus bicycles and I wrote and asked them about the name Linus and the name Gaston and got this reply:

Thank you for your interest in Linus Bikes! Linus is the nephew of one of the company founders. Gaston is a name that embodies the stature of this bike by the way it rides and the classic "cafe racer" style geometry.

Gascony is a place in France and the word Gaston is used by the French when referring to someone from Gascony, a Gaston according to the internet is:

an ecologist at heart who loves nature, animals and the earth. He appreciates simplicity, tranquillity, and is a humble man who loathes shallowness and pretentiousness. Anything out of the ordinary is likely to attract his attention. Although he professes to be a scientific thinker, he could nevertheless be inclined to ponder the big philosophical questions or take an interest in the social sciences or spirituality... When it comes to romance, he is loyal and very loving; and when he falls in love, it will be forever. But cupid had better aim well, because wary and cautious, he doesn't take these things lightly...

Having worked out what the word Gaston means, what is a caff racer? I call them caff racer because that is really how it should be pronounced, the word is spelt café, it's an English working class concept not some pedantic word smith from a university, so I use the English pronunciation. Anyway a caff racer, or the caff racers, were a group of young men and women in the 1950's and 60's in England who got into motorbikes stripped them back to basics and went to caffs and drank tea and ate doughnuts and would do things like put a record on a juke box and race down the street on their bike and try to get back before the record ended, about three minutes. They were also called the Ton Up Boys and they used to do a hundred miles an hour on the, then, new motorways in England, and their bikes, as I said, were stripped back for speed with narrow handlebars.

The term caff racer has now devolved to the bicycle and what it means is a slimmed back retro racing bike with clean lines, no mudguards, underslung North Road handlebars, no chain guards and perhaps a classic slack geometry. I looked up the term classic slack geometry and it is something to do with the angle of the frame to the seat. I also looked up North Road handlebars, they are the old classic swung back handlebars underslung, so pointing downwards rather than up and that is what racers did in the 1930's, North Road was a cycling club in the north of London.

Getting back to bicycle companies, I then found Chappelli in Sydney making really lovely fixed wheel bikes, they also market a ten speed hub geared bike handmade in Italy.

The Chappelli NuVinci infinitely variable hub bicycle which is the product of a collaboration with Fallbrook Technologies. It has been designed specifically for the fashion conscious bicycle aficionado and combines state of the art internal NuVinci hub technology with beautiful handmade bicycle crafting.

The NuVinci sounds like a really interesting bike but for the moment I love my Gaston 3. There are so many new bicycle companies out there it reminds me of the golden age of the bicycle in the 1880's and the 1890's. So if you haven't got one already get yourself a retro or a fixie or a step through with a basket. Let me just add, the step through is not just for girls, if a bloke likes one he can ride it, they are easy to get on and off.

Part Three
Bicycles I Have Known

To School on a Super Elliot

I've owned seven bikes in my life. I learnt to ride on a big old chunky girls' bike, with a classic girls' bike wobble, but that same year I got a racing car red, three speed Super Elliott, semi racer for Christmas with classic swept back handlebars. The bike was for me to use to go to high school but I did much more. My friend Kim and I cycled up Mt Lofty, the local big hill, we had to pedal up 700 steep meters, a fair ride, but coming down was quite a thrill. Kim's bike had a speedometer and he recorded speeds of over forty miles an hour.

When I went to university I abandoned my bike to my brother, he converted it into a chopper. A few years later I found my old Super Elliot semi-racer derelict in an old shed at home so I took the remains of the bike, just a frame really, back to the student house where I lived and rebuilt it. The transformation included new wheels, a new Brooks leather saddle, fixing the Sturmey Archer gears, adding racing drop handlebars, a carrier and I made pannier bags and sprayed it a glorious blue. My old bike had a real makeover and it was now a splendid machine. Cycling up Mt Lofty was no problem. Then one night I was at the theatre, I was into the theatre back then, acting, stage managing, writing plays that sort of thing, and the manager and director wanted to talk to me about a play I had written, I left my bike outside for a moment and when I got back it was gone.

Around Adelaide on a Crannaford

My next bike was built for me by a small company in Adelaide called Crannaford, they were established in the 1940's and made high class bikes. I went around and got measured up and I ordered a steel frame bike, with centre pull brakes, derailleur gears, quick release wheels, drop handlebars and a Brooks saddle and most important of all the colour, I decided to have a yellow bike this time. What a beauty it was, fast with clean lines, no mudguards and I rode up Mt Lofty without blinking. One time I got all the people in our student house to cycle through the Adelaide Hills and down to the Murray River town of Goolwa where we walked along the Coorong, a big sandbar to the Murray mouth. We camped in a field and the next day we raced back to Adelaide.

That bike was my means of transport for years. A popular trip with a girlfriend was to take a train to the Belair National Park, up in the hills, then to speed down back to Adelaide. One day I was cycling through the back streets of Adelaide, I used to cycle through the back doubles as my old Dad called them rather than on main roads, on this occasion I came to a junction and a car suddenly appeared going at a fair pace, I slammed on my brakes and did a complete somersault, I picked myself up and the driver of the car wandered over and said: *I wish I could have got that on film.* My Crannaford was a beautiful bike but in the early eighties I decided to go overseas and I sold my bike and left Australia for some wild adventures around the world.

A Revell in London
Eventually I got to England and went to stay with old student friends in London and David, one of my old friends, told me of a great bike shop in Hampstead, near the famous Hampstead Heath. I found the shop, it looked impressive, I went in and a black man came up to me. When I say black man I don't mean to be disrespectful, he was what the English call West Indian. Now everybody of the old school in England I had met complained that the

blacks were taking over London, so this black man came up to me, more a boy than a man really, and he opened his mouth and spoke. My Dad was born in West Ham and was a real London Cockney, but this black man, when he opened his mouth and spoke, had more of a cockney accent than my dad, I just wanted to laugh, how could anyone be prejudiced against this guy who was obviously just as English, if not more so, than the people who were slagging him off.

He showed me a bike, it was a Revell, a brand of bike built for a group of bike shops in North London by various manufacturers. It had a lightweight frame, I picked it up and it felt really good, smooth and well proportioned. It was a silvery grey with red handlebar tape and black mudguards, it looked very fine and, oh yes, it had a Shimano derailleur with centre pull brakes and quick release wheels. I said I wanted the bike for touring and would need a carrier and a Brooks saddle.
'No worries,' he said.
Well he didn't say *No worries*, he said 'Okie dokie.'
'Good,' I said.
'I'll tell you what, take the bike around the block and if you like it, buy it.'

I could have got on that bike, ridden away and he would have never seen me again and there would have been nothing he could do about it.

'How much is it with the changes?' I said.

He told me, so I took my wallet from my pocket and paid out the money then and there. Someone who was so trusting should be rewarded I felt. The few changes I wanted were done and I rode away across London.

I headed to a suburb called Woolwich, where I was born. I crossed over Tower Bridge, went by the Elephant and Castle pub and on to Greenwich, I knew Greenwich from my childhood with its naval museum, park, international time line and the tea cutter sailing ship the Cutty Sark which is on show there.

I came alongside another cyclist named John and we chatted as we rode side by side, I asked him the direction to Woolwich, the next town along the River Thames, then I was hit by a truck. I was lifted up, thrown down, my brand new bike collapsed under me and I landed on my hand. John was down as well. Time seemed to stand still as I sprawled on the road with traffic coming at me from all directions. I stood up, tottered and nearly fell. I picked up my bike, John helped me, and the driver of the truck helped too. He gave me his address and John gave me his address, I told them I was okay and not to worry and then I found myself alone on the side of a busy road with a bike with buckled wheels and a right hand that didn't work anymore.

Luckily the bike was lightweight. I threw it over my shoulder, walked to the closest bike shop, left the bike and then walked to the local hospital. There a nice Sri Lankan nurse looked after me and I was x-rayed and bandaged up, about three bones in my right hand were broken. A week later I was back. I picked up my repaired bike and cycled all the way across London from Greenwich, in the East End, to Walton on Thames in Surrey. It was an epic ride. My right hand didn't work so it was very hard to change gears, I couldn't use the right hand front brake and London is a very busy town full of traffic! I just dropped my right hand over the handlebars to give me a bit of stability and kept going.

I stayed in Walton on Thames for a week and then, with my useless right hand, I cycled 500 miles from London to Ramsgate, on to Dover and then from Dover via London to Land's End in Cornwall.

On Tour to Oxford

I spent a couple of summers working in a youth hostel in Swanage and from there I took several cycling tours, I visited the Isle of Wight, Oxford, Bath, Dartmoor again and Scotland, but it was the Oxford trip that is burnt into my psych. My Australian friend who lived in London, Michele, wanted to meet me in Oxford, she was to take the train with her bike as she only had a day free and I would cycle as I could manage three days. All was arranged and bright and early one morning I swung onto my bike, pedalled around to the Poole ferry, crossed and headed north to Salisbury. That part of the trip was easy, just pure leg work. I swung through Salisbury and was going north up a hill in a medium gear, I didn't need low gears, most of the time my iron thighs could easily propel me forward, I pedalled up hill, no problem, listening for cars as I always do. A car overtook me, he gave me plenty of room, no problem again, but he was towing a caravan and he cut in front of me. I saw it coming, this great wall of white, actually I think the bottom of the caravan was silver as some are, chrome or something, and in a massively slow moment the caravan careered towards me and with one ginormous slap swept up my whole body and my bike and threw us down, it was a terrifying experience.

I was left grovelling in the road as the offending vehicle sped away. My whole side was grazed, I was miles from anywhere, I was abandoned, lying in the road with a dead bike. I staggered to my feet, there was nothing I could do about the bleeding apart from letting it stop naturally, I picked up my bike, threw it over my shoulder and with a badly buckled bike and bleeding legs and arms I somehow managed to hitch a lift back to Salisbury! I was dropped at the edge of town and walked to a bike shop and checked my poor machine in for major surgery, then I walked to the hospital where an Indian nurse took charge of me. A couple of hours later I emerged from the hospital wrapped up like an Egyptian Mummy. I caught a train to Oxford to meet Michele. I checked into the youth hostel that night and lay in agony not really being able to sleep as my side hurt.

Oxford was great, in spite of my lack of a bike, Michele and I wandered all over the old university colleges and along the Thames and had afternoon tea in a quaint Ye Olde Worlde Tea Shoppe. The next day I trained back to Salisbury, picked up my bike and still with a very much broken body cycled back to Swanage.

An Abandoned Relic in Yorkshire

After three years, and some memorable rides, a few of which come at the end of the book if you want a good read, I sold my touring bike and went back to Australia via India. Six months later I was off again, I flew to China and from there made my way overland back to England. In England I settled for a time in Yorkshire. I worked in a pub in the Yorkshire Dales called The Nelson Inn near Harrogate, The Nellie was what everybody called it. I rode an old red fold up bike to and from work every day, it wasn't much fun climbing from the valleys up into *them there hills* on a fold up bike, the gears seemed better suited to the flat, but it was a lovely ride. I remember having to charge down a hill and circle around and up a tree lined road and the farmers were all hay making and, believe it or not, for a week or two in England the sun shone.

The fold up bike was always hard to propel probably due to its small wheels. Small wheels or not I rode it until the cavalry arrived. Propped up against a dry stone wall I found an abandoned dropped handlebar, black bike, it was unrideable but

I took it home and greased and oiled it, fixed up the Sturmey Archer gears, bought new tubes and tyres, got new handlebar tape, added a carrier, a new saddle, fixed the breaks and, Bob's your uncle, I had a very rideable machine.

I often rode around a town called Penny Pot and I rode through the Dales from Harrogate to Leeds and later across the Pennines from Leeds to Stockport. I was studying to be a teacher in Stockport at the time and I rode to college every day and up into the Pennines when I was posted as a trainee teacher in the mountains. I remember early one morning charging down a particularly steep hill and turning to climb another, the traffic was busy and speeding by, I was cruising along a riverbank with winter trees lining its banks, it was very cold and black ice was on the road, I didn't see it and over I went but no harm done I stood up, righted my bike and carried on.

My most memorable ride on the old relic I found propped up against a wall was going home to Cheadle, where I lived, from the outskirts of Manchester, where my teacher training college was. It had been snowing overnight, the council workers had cleared the roads but to the side of the road were great snow drifts. I plodded along carefully, there was a car behind me but it was being quite cautious as there wasn't enough room to pass, the snow drifts hedged us in. Suddenly an old lady, in a Mini, overtook the car behind me and then hit me full on broadside. I was thrown full force into a great drift of snow. I got up and shook myself off and this rickety old lady wanted to know if I was okay. My bike was badly shaken, I was badly shaken but as I had been wearing a thick down jacket, gloves, a beanie and thick trousers I was shaken but not stirred. I picked up my bike, carried it to the nearest bike shop and left it there to be repaired. I then took my down jacket to a dry cleaners, the jacket was white and the snow had been stained black by road grime so it needed a good clean, then I walked home. For once I had been in a crash on my bike where only my pride was hurt, my body had come off unscathed.

Another time I worked as a storeman for Marks and Spencer in Leeds, teaching hadn't agreed with me, and I had to get up sometime around 4am to get to work. It was pitch black and very cold, the season was getting on for Christmas. I mounted my bike, dressed in a big down jacket I had bought in China, thick gloves, thick socks, boots, scarf and a beanie, and I cycled off into the darkness. It wasn't just cold and it wasn't just dark, there was a hoarfrost and tiny particles of ice filled the air suspended in the atmosphere. As I rode along my jacket and trouser legs collected and became layered in the ice particles, as did my face. It was cold, it was ice cold, as I battled on through the very early morning darkness to get to work.

A Ricardo to Belair

After three years in England I returned to Australia with Sue, who later became my wife. We acquired two ten speed, bright red Ricardo bikes. Mine had a white seat and white handlebar tape and actually looked good, Sue's was a red step through girls' bike with a basket, a carrier and mudguards but we didn't buy them, that is we didn't buy them from a shop, we got them from a friend of Sue's who didn't want them anymore. The bikes were great but too small for us really bikes, like shoes, need to be the right size. We used to take the train up to Belair National Park in Adelaide and cycle around the park and then come speeding home downhill from about 700 meters above sea level to the sea at Henley Beach where we lived. It was on one of these downhill jaunts that Sue called out to me:

'My brakes aren't working!'

I replied: 'Yes they are, you just aren't using them properly.'

'My brakes are not working!'

'Just use them as I showed you not putting them on too tight and releasing them and putting them on again.'

All this was being said as we charged downhill.

'I tried that and they don't work.'

'Stupid woman.'

'Don't call me a stupid woman.'

'Just do as I said.'

'I did.'

'Okay, stop and we will swap bikes.'

We swapped bikes, I charged off on Sue's, I put the brakes on and nothing happened, the bloody brakes weren't working and the only way I could stop myself was by crashing into a box hedge. Sue cracked up laughing.

'You stupid idiot why didn't you tell me the brakes didn't work?' I said.

A Mountain Bike to Nowhere

One night my brother needed some help transporting two mountain bikes from his workshop to his house in Glenelg, I volunteered. *What beautiful, brilliantly geared machines these are,* I thought, as we casually cruised through Glenelg, *I want one of these.* So I went out and bought one, my very first mountain bike. I took it up to our 100 acre property in Burra, later to become our cider farm, and rode it around once and hated it! I stood it on the verandah of our house and left it there. One day I was working down the road so I took the bike in the back of our ute and told Sue that when I had finished I'd cycle home. Cycling up hill and down dale on that mountain bike was very hard work, it was beautifully geared but I couldn't get any speed up, cycling was slow and painful, I don't think the small 26inch wheels helped. I gave the thing away.

The Back Streets of Burra on a Gaston 3

After my shemozzle with a mountain bike I gave cycling away. Then one day I saw a Pashley Guv'nor on a British TV show and fell in love. I never did get that Pashley Guv'nor, I ran out of money, but I did get a Linus Gaston 3 with a lightweight frame and a 3 speed Sturmey Archer hub. It's black with white wheels and Linus's own version of North Road handlebars and it is stylish to say the least and very beautiful. Sue got a Linus mixte, rosewood in colour, step through with an upright sitting position and she loves her bike too.

Every day, when we lived in Burra, we got up early before the traffic and the kids went to school, and cycled downhill the kilometre of dirt track that was our road down to the bitumen. Sue went steadily and I give her a head start and then I sped downhill crashing by. We cycled into town across a narrow double humped bridge and turned onto the bike track and then we cruised along the Burra Creek by the old abandoned smelters, Burra is a heritage copper mining town, then we passed the old police station and turned up to the old jail. The road up to the jail is a slow steady climb, after the jail the road continues to get steeper and steeper all the way up to the ghost town of Hampton.

It was at Hampton that the ride became really interesting. We had brilliant views of the old Burra mine across the fields, it had been a bit of a push to get there so we would stop and enjoy the view as the sun came up, very beautiful. The ride down back into Burra was exhilarating, the road tumbles down the hill with a tight right turn and we used to speed through open grazing country back to civilisation.

Twice however on our ride I collected a three cornered jack, a rather lethal local seed that is a thorn ridden death trap for bicycle tubes. It is every cyclists nightmare. Still the daily cycle up to Hampton did wonders for our leg and arm muscles and Sue says it was great for the breathing and ones stamina went through the roof.

Part Four
Books on Bicycles

The Wheels of Chance 1895

HG Wells wrote science fiction at the start of the twentieth century and produced such classics as *The War of The Worlds* and *The Time Machine.* He also loved bikes and in two of his famous social novels *The History of Mr Poly* and *Kips* the hero discovers the love of his life while riding a safety bicycle. In Kips the hero's friend, Sid, made: *the best machines at a democratic price in London,* they cost: *Pantocrat tyres eight pound – clinchers ten – Dunlops eleven – ladies one pound more –* A Pantocrat is either a brand or type of tyre, I'm wondering if they were a solid rubber tyre as solid tyres were cheaper than Dunlops. Clinchers are the same as for modern bike wheels with a ridge either side to clinch the tyre in place, Dunlops refers to modern tyres which have a tube to inflate the tyre and therefore provide an air cushion and give a comfortable ride. The wheels with inflatable tyres and the chains with different sized cogs were the two innovations that made cycling popular and basically led to the safety bicycle which is the prototype for all modern bikes.

The Wheels of Chance is Wells first book and it is indeed a book on cycling. Chapter one is really about learning to ride, HG Wells seems to have had some difficulty, and Hoopdriver, the hero, comes off rather badly, his legs are badly bruised and his body is battered. In spite of his injuries Hoopdriver cycles off into the dawn on a bicycle tour of southern England. *He did not ride fast, he did not ride straight, an exacting critic might say he did not ride well – but he rode generously, opulently, using the whole road and even nibbling at the footpath.*

Three Men on the Bummel 1914
This is a sequel to *Three Men in a Boat*, which I must add is brilliant, but I can't say the same for *Three Men on the Bummel*. What is the bummel you ask? The bummel is a meander on a bicycle, or on foot, or by train, to nowhere in particular. The bummel of the book is a cycling tour of Germany, mostly it isn't about cycling, but Germany comes up big. The cycling bits are the best part of the book and there is some brilliant stuff on all the newfangled, all singing and dancing furphies and whizzbangs that you could then buy for your bike, and bike shops are still stuffed with them today. In one section the author writes about saddles and

concludes: *There may be a better land where --- saddles are made out of rainbows, stuffed with cloud; in this world the simplest thing is to get used to something hard.* You must also look out for the section on the mechanical cycling enthusiast, he gets the front wheel off and strips out the ball bearings, losing a few in the process, gets the gears off and loses the screws and then finds it almost impossible to get the bike back together, and check out the section on cycling posters, the book is really worth a skim.

Richard's Bicycle Book 1975
This book is a classic. I first read it in the late 1970's and learnt a lot about cycling and how to use my ten speed derailleur racing bike properly. Now there is a new version out, I've picked up Richards 21st Century Bicycle Book and it is crammed full of stuff, even more so than the original, and is the bicycle book you must read if you want to really start getting into the technical side of cycling. Richard's book is like a big meal, it takes time to digest, and in addition to the technical and mechanical data it is full of the 1970's hippyish: taking on the establishment and winning, bikes are good, bikes are environmentally sound, cars are bad, let's hang together and save the world by cycling.

There is nothing wrong with these sentiments, they are all true, but these days…well the fight has been lost for the moment, cars are ever increasing in numbers but at the same time bikes are more popular than ever so it isn't total defeat, and rationalisation of city transport, including the bike, is slowly coming about. I live in the world we have and see bikes as just plain fun and exhilarating and great excitement machines and if bikes can be seen that way then they will always have a future.

Getting back to Richard's Bicycle Book, to me he has a 1970's love of derailleur gears, that they are just so much better than hub gears, having used both I like hub gears and I think ninety percent of cyclists could use hub gears effectively whereas only about ten percent of cyclists actually know how to use their derailleurs. Here is what Richard says: *There are two broad kinds of transmission internal hub gears and external derailleur gears. In general hub gears are simple, reliable, and a bit slow, and derailleur gears are more complex, need more frequent servicing, and are extremely efficient – fast.*

Bike Snob 2010

Really this book is about bike culture in New York. It purports to be about many things but it is basically about all the cycling sub cultures in the author's home town. Having said that the section called Velo-Taxonomy is quite the best bit and reminds me of the famous characters written throughout time starting a long time ago by some Greek or other. One of the characters in this book is The Roadie. The Roadie is the lycra clad carbon fibre biked road racer and Bike Snob writes: *Beneath all the training and suffering and lycra and embrocations, the fact is that all Roadies are freeloading cheats.* Bike Snob goes on to write: *The Roadies life is full of disappointed people – Spouses, friends, family – all of whom have involuntarily funded their depraved life style…*

Just Ride 2012

I read this book of short little chapters and my wife did the same and we both thoroughly enjoyed it. The author talks of his experiences and his conversion from a lycra clad racer charging around on carbon fibre misfits to a rational cyclist who uses his bike to get to work and to go on weekend twenty four hour cycling jaunts. There is much good stuff in this book and a whole philosophy of cycling that needs to be read by the carbon fibre cowboys out there, no, it needs to be read by anybody thinking of getting a bike. About gears the author states: *You have way too many gears....you need eight gears.* Just Ride is a good read, perhaps a must read, for all those getting into the cycling lark.

The Bicycle Owners Handbook 2012
This is a do-it-yourself bicycle maintenance book, it is more basic than I was looking for but hey if you have just bought a bike and don't know how to look after it at all, including greasing your chain and fixing a puncture, you need this book. There is a nice quote in there somewhere: *Cleaning your bike can be a very satisfying experience, as well as a valuable one. Dirty bikes are just less pleasant to ride – the chain will wear down quicker and the gears will be slow to shift. A proper 25 minute clean will keep it running smooth and looking sharp.*

Cycle Chic 2012
If you want to see pictures, lots of pictures, of well dressed people ridings bikes try this. The author or photographer is dead against lycra and cycle wear, he is into using your cycle for enjoyment and to get from A to B, he is also into mudguards and baskets. He lives in Copenhagen, which is considered one of

the cycling cities of the world alongside Amsterdam, so cycling there is a different matter to charging around congested and busy London on one's treadly. I have done that and paid for my sins.

Part Five
Blokes on Bikes

Mulga Bill's Bicycle 1896

There is a famous, famous in Australia, poem about a bike ride, *Mulga Bill's Bicycle*, written by the Australian poet Banjo Paterson in1896:

'TWAS Mulga Bill, from Eaglehawk, that caught the cycling craze;
He turned away the good old horse that served him many days;
He dressed himself in cycling clothes, resplendent to be seen;
He hurried off to town and bought a shining new machine;
And as he wheeled it through the door, with air of lordly pride,
The grinning shop assistant said, *Excuse me, can you ride?*
See here, young man, said Mulga Bill, *from Walgett to the sea,*
From Conroy's Gap to Castlereagh, there's none can ride like me.
I'm good all round at everything, as everybody knows,

Although I'm not the one to talk - I hate a man that blows.
But riding is my special gift, my chiefest, sole delight;
Just ask a wild duck can it swim, a wild cat can it fight.
There's nothing clothed in hair or hide, or built of flesh or steel,
There's nothing walks or jumps, or runs, on axle, hoof or wheel,
But what I'll sit, while hide will hold and girths and straps are tight;
I'll ride this here two-wheeled concern right straight away at sight.
'Twas Mulga Bill, from Eaglehawk, that sought his own abode,
That perched above the Dead Man's Creek, beside the mountain road.
He turned the cycle down the hill and mounted for the fray,
But ere he'd gone a dozen yards it bolted clean away.
It left the track, and through the trees, just like a silver streak,
It whistled down the awful slope towards the Dead Man's Creek.

It shaved a stump by half an inch, it dodged a big white-box:
The very wallaroos in fright went scrambling up the rocks,
The wombats hiding in their caves dug deeper underground,
But Mulga Bill, as white as chalk, clung tight to every bound.
It struck a stone and gave a spring that cleared a fallen tree,
It raced beside a precipice as close as close could be;
And then, as Mulga Bill let out one last despairing shriek,
It made a leap of twenty feet into the Dead Man's Creek.
'Twas Mulga Bill, from Eaglehawk, that slowly swam ashore:
He said, *I've had some narrer shaves and lively rides before;*
I've rode a wild bull round a yard to win a five-pound bet,
But that was sure the derndest ride that I've encountered yet.
I'll give that two-wheeled outlaw best; it's shaken all my nerve

To feel it whistle through the air and plunge and buck and swerve.
It's safe at rest in Dead Man's Creek - we'll leave it lying still;
A horse's back is good enough henceforth for Mulga Bill.

In fact it turned out to be the horse that got retired and the bicycle is still with us.

Left for Dead 1930's
My Dad's bicycle was a Raleigh with Sturmey Archer gears, he bought it with the money from his paper round and paid sixpence a week, this was in the 1930's. One day he got on his bike and got Stan, his young brother who had a small bike, to go for a ride and they cycled all the way from the East End of London to Ramsgate, on the south coast of England, and back. Dad got into trouble for taking Stan so far. Dad was always a bit of a wanderer, enjoying travel and seeing new places and that is why he joined the Royal Navy in World War Two and later he took his family across the world to Australia.

My brothers and sisters and I were lucky that we were ever born. Dad was run down twice, once when he was a toddler and a second time on his bike and then in World War Two, he was in the Royal Navy, and his ship was nearly sunk twice. It rammed and sank a German cruiser and sailed home backwards at three knots as German Aircraft flew in circles overhead, they couldn't attack because they couldn't see the ship due to Nordic fog. On a second occasion Dad's ship was torpedoed by an Italian submarine and was dead in the water when a squadron of Italian Torpedo planes attacked, luckily every torpedo missed, but I digress, I am writing here about Dad's big cycle accident, he told me the story in a fish and chip café on the beach front in Adelaide:

'I was listening to a boxing match on the radio between Joe Louis and Tommy Far, a Welsh heavyweight boxing champion, I was a bit late getting out on my way to work, this happened in an area called the Abbey Arms near where I was run over as a kid, I was meant to be at work at 7.30. At the Abbey Arms it was a big junction all buses lined up and trams, they used to run up the embankment and down, I was stopped in the middle of the road on my bike behind a tram that had stopped and the next tram behind me couldn't brake. As the tram hit me I went through the back window of the tram in front and came out the other side and ended up under a bus in the curb. There was a crowd there and a couple of blokes and women pulled me out stood me up, *I'm right now*, I said. *Come and sit in the tram*, they said. I tried to step up and I couldn't go anymore 'cause all my ribs were broken. They were shooing people off the tram so I could sit there till an ambulance came.

I was seventeen, this happened end of November, they took me to Queen Mary Hospital in Stratford first and there they thought I wouldn't make it through the night, I had fractured ribs, two broken collar bones and I was bleeding internally, so they took me to Whips Cross Sanatorium. They didn't tell me, I heard them telling Mum, it was somewhere where they took people for the last couple of days before they die. Whips Cross blinking good hospital treated me well I couldn't eat or drink, had to have a nurse to do anything. I didn't die, they let me out for Christmas, they told me I wasn't to do anything, if I went to the toilet I had to have someone with me. After Christmas I went back and was in there for another month. After that Mum had to take me to Whips Cross eight miles away every day. I wasn't allowed to get up and down on a tram on my own.'

Poor old Dad was in a bad way but he pulled through and with the insurance money he bought a car, a Ford Eight and Hitler invaded Poland and World War Two began. I'm not sure if Dad buying a Ford Eight caused World War Two however, let's just say the jury is still out on that one.

The Skegness Wheelers Cycling Club 1938 – Dennis Cox

The joy of cycling is certainly apparent in this extract from Dennis Cox's autobiography.

'It was about this time that I got involved with a cycling club. I had been approached by a rather attractive young red-headed lass who lived not far from us, her name was Esme Crow and she belonged to the Skegness Wheelers Cycling Club. I was very shy in those days and made the excuse that I didn't have a suitable bicycle. She kept asking me and I kept putting her off. Anyway, one day I went to the small garage just round the corner from where we lived, for a recharge for our radio. I walked through the showroom on my way out and there I noticed a second hand racing bike for sale. It looked in very good condition and it was just my size. The price was thirty shillings. I couldn't afford to pay for it outright but the garage proprietor's wife, who looked after the financial side of the business, said I could pay a small deposit and the balance at so much per week over so many weeks. I was delighted. Closer examination of the machine revealed that it was a Raleigh Record, a very good quality bike. It was a fixed gear, painted black with the name in gold letters on the down tube.

The first time Esme saw me out on this bike she pounced on me and this time I had no excuse. She persuaded me to go out for a trial run with the club and if I didn't like it she wouldn't bother me again. The following Sunday morning Esme called for me as arranged and we rode the few miles to Burgh-le-Marsh where we were to meet the club on a ride from Skegness to the Lincolnshire Wolds. I was introduced to the various riders, I can't remember how many there were on that occasion but they seemed a nice cheerful group and I was made very welcome. My initial nervousness soon disappeared and I settled down to enjoy the ride. Some of the riders passed favourable comments on my bike and gave me advice on riding position, suitable clothing and so on.

Our destination that day was the little village of Donington-on-Bain where we stopped for lunch. I don't remember where else we went but I do know I thoroughly enjoyed it and was sorry when we arrived back at Burgh-le-Marsh where Esme and I left the group to make our way home. From then on I was hooked and I joined the club. We went out every Sunday, hail, rain or shine. We often met up with other clubs from various places at the lunch or tea stops. These were usually cafes that catered especially for cyclists. They allowed you to consume your own food and drink if you wished or like me, couldn't afford to buy it. Often there would be scores of bicycles parked outside a cafe in a village or small town. Often we would pass other clubs on the road to somewhere and we would all sing out a greeting, *Hi-de-hi*. The other club would reply *Ho-de-ho*. There was a good spirit of camaraderie among cyclists in those days. There was a great attitude in the Skegness Wheelers too. On club rides the motto was:

The speed of the group is the speed of the slowest rider.

Everyone kept together, and if any one got a puncture or had other mechanical trouble the whole group stopped until the problem was fixed. Young riders were nursed along and encouraged as were new riders whatever their age. I was always sorry when Sundays came to an end.'

A Hercules Racer Late 40's & early 50's – Eric Sanderson

My Uncle-in-law, if there is such a thing, definitely loved his cycling.

'There were some good amateur cyclists in Leeds in the late 1940's, but most of us started off with a second hand bike, usually of a fairly robust and heavy construction, which was used to get around and explore the district and even further afield before becoming more serious about the sport. One lad whose father was a butcher, used to ride a delivery boy's bike with the basket on the front. For myself, my first grown up bike, pride and joy was a well-worn Hercules with a 3 speed derailleur gear. It was many years later before I acquired a lightweight racing bike, assembled piece by piece from the savings of my Sunday morning paper round.

I always preferred a freewheel bike, where you could recover some of the energy expended by coasting down the other side of the hill you'd just battled to conquer. The fixed wheel style consumed more energy and was more suited to winter training. I found it exhausting and dangerous, probably due to my attention span resembling that of a greenfly and forgetting to keep my legs spinning the pedals. This caused me to become unsteady with many a resultant tumble.

Before becoming involved in club cycling, three or four of us would make regular Sunday rides to destinations like Helmsley, Skipton, York, there was a bizarre cycle track alongside the main road. One occasion saw us riding into a strong headwind, intent on reaching Helmsley. We tired well short of our target, at a village called Oswaldkirk, and decided to retire to the local pub for a pint or so to recover some of our stamina, confident that the strong headwind that had defeated us would help push us home in record speed. Unfortunately, meteorology often displays a stubborn resistance to follow amateur logic and emerging from a happy lunchtime session we found that the wind had turned through 180 degrees. However, feeling suitably refreshed by a generous libation of the local bitter, we confidently started our return journey, only to find that far from reinvigorating our depleted energy levels, the drinking session had sapped our few reserves such that we could barely make any headway into the oncoming gale. A seemingly endless nightmare ensued where we seriously contemplated spending the night in a convenient hedgerow and when we finally arrived home, utterly exhausted, I believe the air sea rescue teams were on the point of being alerted and only just avoided scrambling their helicopters. A hard learned lesson: never drink and ride a bike.'

A Malvern Star Dragster 1970's – Colin Thorogood

Those first heady moments at Christmas on one's brand new bicycle. Unforgettable.

'My first memories of riding bicycles started at the tender age of seven when I received my first bicycle, a dragster. It was a beautiful blue Malvern Star with large handlebars, it had a long red banana seat, it also had a tall chromed sissybar rising into the heavens and it had a T bar gear shifter on the cross bar that showed 3 gears. I remember quite vividly the feelings of excitement and joy, they were overwhelming. The feeling of being mobile was so liberating. All my expectations were fulfilled when I first sat on that red banana seat, placing my feet on those peddles and pushing down on them. I was off.

I had motion. As I moved off I could feel the adrenalin rushing through my body and my heart pounding in my chest. I was gone. Before I knew it, I had ridden all the way to the end of the street!

I can still remember the feelings I experienced when I was at the end of the street and looked back at my parents, my sisters and brothers. They were all there standing outside our house, they looked so far away. I had gained my freedom. I rode my bicycle everywhere especially down to the local creek which was a labyrinth of eucalyptus trees, willow trees, bamboo, and papyri. It was a real swamp, my new playground, where all the kids from the surrounding neighbourhood would gather to do battle. Such fun we had. At the end of those wonderful days I would go back to my best friend's home to relive the accounts of that day. They were some of the most wonderful days of my childhood.

I rode my bike to school every day for four years and then one day I went to retrieve it from the bike racks and it was gone. My bike was nowhere to be seen. I was shattered.'

Basingstoke's Sleeping Beauty – Jason Dennes
Rather Jason than me!

'I used to cycle to work, left the house 7.15am, one winter it was still really dark and I was wrapped up really warm (snug as a bug). My route took me across some fields and halfway across one I fell asleep, I woke up as I hit the ground. Took me a minute to figure out where I was and what had happened, very scary. I reckon I must be the only person to fall asleep whilst cycling.'

Part Six
Girls on Wheels

The Early Days

It seems silly now but girls had one hell of a time getting on bicycles. They weren't allowed to show their ankles, bikes were considered bad for a woman's health, women with muscles were considered unfeminine, riding bikes, it was said, interfered with the female reproductive organs and also that girls who rode bikes took up immoral acts.

Thankfully many writers considered the bicycle was good for women's health, that it got them out of the house and away from chaperones, and the doldrums, and many women writers thought of the bicycle as a great step forward for the liberation of women. It meant taking up the wearing of sensible dress, at this time women still wore high necks, long full dresses, with high heeled boots and worst of all corsets that stopped them from breathing properly, interfered with circulation and were especially bad for pregnant women. In the end the proponents of rational dress and the bicycle won but not without a fight.

The penny farthing, the bicycle with one giant wheel at the front and one small wheel at the back, was considered too dangerous for women and how could they ride with all those acres of dress? The truth is the penny farthing was also too dangerous for men, an alternative was needed.

The Step Through 1889
Bicycles with no top bar, where instead the bar curved up and thus the bike could be stepped through, were built especially for ladies as they wore long full on dresses, and with this new design, as opposed to the standard diamond frame, girls could easily ride a bike in the more formal Victorian era. These bikes often came with a skirt guard on the back wheel, a sort of a net to keep the dress from getting caught in the spokes, and often had a full chain guard again to protect the ladies dress. The handlebars were positioned high and swung back and this gave the rider a comfortable upright position and the saddle was often sprung and soft with a snub nose, again so that the ladies dress could easily fall forward. Another difference with the step through was that they often had a rear coaster brake that was operated from the peddles.

Today girls wear jeans and can ride any bike suitable to their build and as girls are not so fond of showing off in the way men are, they often go for utility and the step through has had a big revival. With rubber peddles and the traditional step through design girls can dress up and still cycle and look smart as opposed to the sweaty men in their lycra. One video clip I saw had boys showing off on their multi coloured streamlined fixies with the girls watching on, all equipped with step through bikes in lovely soft colours, upright riding positions, swung back handlebars, three speed gears, mud guards, rear carriers and a basket. You can even get flowers to decorate the basket!

In post World War Two England and America the step through fell out of fashion but in Holland it has been manufactured since 1911 to a standard pattern with single speed, 28inch tyres, black frame and mudguards with a skirt guard on the back wheel, they are called Omafiets or Grannies bike. The Dutch also have the equivalent in a gent's bike and this is why these sort of retro bikes are often called Dutch bikes. I have to admit that in the plethora of pastel colours the step throughs now come in, with baskets and flowers they do look rather lovely, they look happy and a joy to ride, which can't be said for the carbon fibre extrusions of the racing fraternity.

So who invented the step through and should we put up a statue to him or her? In the 1890's there was a lot of mud thrown at women cyclist, not literally but verbally, and also in print, and bicycle companies needed to come up with a solution of how to get women on wheels in a socially acceptable way. A gent, a weird inventor fellow named James Starley came up with the solution in 1889 or to be more precise, the company he set up which was inherited by his sons and at that time run by them, came up with the solution.

In 1889, the Starley Brothers introduced the psycho ladies bicycle, which had a step through frame and tackled the modesty problem by forcing the cyclist to sit bolt upright. The psycho ladies bicycle of 1889 looks exactly, well not exactly, but it does look pretty much like a girls step through bike of today. The psycho tag had nothing to do with the ladies bike, it was in fact the name of the Starley Brothers range of bikes and took its name from a magician's automaton. The ladies psycho was a black step through with swing back handlebars, mud guards, a full chain guard and a rear wheel net to protect dresses from getting entangled, it had it all.

Emancipation 1890's

In the 1890's the safety bicycle became all the rage, it was a golden age of cycling and was taken up by women. In America a famous feminist Susan B Anthony described the safety bicycle as *The Freedom Machine*, she said:

Let me tell you what I think of bicycling. I think it has done more to emancipate women than anything else in the world. It gives women a feeling of freedom and self-reliance. I stand and rejoice every time I see a woman ride by on a wheel...the picture of free, untrammelled womanhood.

How I learnt to Ride a Bicycle 1891

Frances E Willard was a big deal in the late nineteenth century feminist movement. In those days if you were a feminist you didn't burn your bra and cut your hair short, you went to church and looked and acted like a pillar of society and using this technique Frances Willard was able to achieve many things. If a woman rode a bicycle she was considered radical and would be the butt of chauvinist jokes and if she wore bloomers and sensible dress she was considered a prostitute, the clothes women of the day had to wear were appalling. In some US cities it was illegal for women to ride bikes, some places also made it illegal for women to wear bloomers, bloomers are a sort of baggy dress like trousers, and bicycles encouraged women to dress sensibly. So the mere fact that Francis Willard learnt to ride a bike and wrote a book about it was, at the time, a bit radical. Incidentally the book was a best seller. There is a lot of good quotable stuff in this little book so here goes:

Behold, I do not fail you... said the bicycle instructor teaching Frances how to ride...*You must now learn the laws of balance and exploitation...Strange as the paradox might seem you will do your best by not trying to do it at all...Look up and off and on and out; get forehead and foot into line, the latter acting as a rhythmic spur into the flanks of your equilibriated equine; so shall you win and that right speedily.*

I called her Gladys... she refers here to her step through safety bike, *having in view the exhilarating motion of the machine, and the gladdening effect of its acquaintance...*

I finally concluded that all failure was from a wobbling will rather than a wobbling wheel.

We saw that the physical development of humanity's mother-half would be wonderfully advanced by the universal introduction of the bicycle…

I don't do Francis justice, get hold of the little book and have a read, in a sense the book should be called how not to learn to ride a bike. For a better way to learn how to ride a bicycle get hold of the book *Just Ride*.

Daisy 1892
There are some great songs about bikes such as *A Bicycle Made for Two,* written in 1892.

Daisy Daisy, give me an answer true
I'm half crazy over the love of you
It won't be a stylish marriage
I can't afford a carriage
But you'll look sweet
Upon the seat
Of a bicycle made for two.

This song has an interesting story to it. Harry Dacre, an Englishman and a popular composer, travelled to the United States, he took with him a bicycle and was charged import duty. At the time another songwriter said, *It's lucky you didn't bring a bicycle built for two, otherwise you'd have to pay double duty,* and Harry Dacre took the phrase *bicycle built for two* and composed a song around it. The song was a success in the London music halls, and in America it was a hit when sung by Jennie Lindsay at the Atlantic Gardens on the Bowery in 1892.

Sensible Dress 1895
I read HG Wells book *The Wheels of Change* and then re-read it. The second time around I picked up on what sort of get up the Lady in Grey, the heroine, was wearing and the fuss that was made of her cycling costume. Her costume was described by Wells as knickerbockers, which I take it to mean something like bloomers, and he also describes how she was wearing a button up skirt, a button up skirt apparently is a full skirt that can be turned into something like trousers, of course this caused the hero a spot of bother later on when the Lady in Grey was insulted, not to her face, and he stepped in and defended her honour. At that time it seems that if a girl wore sensible dress she was labelled a whore

but the bicycle was too brilliant an invention to stand for such nonsense and wearing sensible dress and girls on wheels were an unstoppable phenomena.

According to Wikipedia: *Knickerbockers are a form of men's or boys baggy kneed trousers and golfers often wore them.*

Mapp and Lucia 1939

In *Trouble For Lucia,* one of the series of books featuring Mapp and Lucia written by EF Benson and published in 1939, Lucia the Italianophile heroine suddenly gets interested in bicycles. Lucia and Georgie, her limp wristed consort, hire bikes that are secretly taken out to country lanes were they learn to ride. *...they wobbled about the road with uncalculable swoopings...* and Lucia, trying very hard to avoid him twice, manages to crash into a man painting telegraph poles with tar. Lucia and Georgie master the art of bike riding and then they order two brand new machines. *The bicycles arrived a week later, nickel-plated and belled and braked.*

Later in the book Lucia gets booked for cycling downhill at twenty miles an hour, she couldn't find the brakes only the bell, and sent people fleeing as she charged downhill ringing the bell, as a result of the court case Tilling, the local town, goes cycling mad. *It became fashionable to career up and down the high street after dark, when traffic was diminished, and the whole length of it resounded with tinkling bells and twinkled with bicycle lamps.* Then people became more adventurous, A*s the days grew longer and the weather warmer, picnic parties were arranged to points of interest within easy distance…and they ate sandwiches and drank from their thermos-flasks in ruined dungeons or on tombstones or by the edge of a moat!*

Dinah's Engagement Ring 1940's – Brenda Sanderson

Bicycle clubs were all the go before the motor car edged them off the road and it seems that joining a bicycle club was a good way to court a young lady or a young man in the 1940's & 50's.

Dinah, my wife's mother, met her man, so to speak, through a cycling club. Dinah's sister Brenda wrote, 'Dinah was always a private person, even as a young woman and I think she had very few boyfriends up to meeting Bill. They were introduced by Dinah's school friends Rita and Olive Scadden who in turn were friends of Bill's cycling group and

I remember Dinah joining the cycling club which Bill was already a long standing member of. He had a heavy touring bike and the first longish ride your Mum went on resulted in a very sore bum, aching legs and a painful sunburn. I don't think it was her favourite pastime.

Bill was a keen cyclist, I'm told he had a Rudge touring bike fitted with Sturmey Archer gears, and he and his club mates used to roam far and wide, into the Dales - Skipton, Grassington, Upper Wharfedale and Swaledale as well as out into the East Riding of Yorkshire - Helmsley, Ampleforth, Teesdale and so on. Dinah didn't have a bike 'til sometime after she met Bill and cycling wasn't her favourite pastime. She joined up because of Bill's interest but Dinah was less enthusiastic and their joint excursions were much more modest, limited to the back roads to Otley, Knaresborough, Wetherby and the like. Her bike was, if I remember correctly, a Raleigh. Dinah joined up because of Bill's interest and a few of her other friends were also in the cycling club. She used to find it very hard to keep up with the more enthusiastic cyclists, especially on the longer runs and wasn't unhappy when they gave it up. I seem to recollect that Bill sold his bike to fund Dinah's engagement ring.'

Near Miss 1960 – Pam Harrison

I have written this book as if riding a bike is the most natural thing ever, like a duck taking to water, but cycling, especially on modern roads full of cars trying to get nowhere very fast, isn't for everyone as Pam's story indicates.

'I remember once cycling down a hill and the bike going too fast so I applied the brakes all the way down the lane. It joined a major road at the bottom and my hands were sort of locked and I couldn't brake anymore so had to jump off or would have been under a car. That put me off bikes for life!'

Tangled in the Brambles 1960's – Alison Whish

My friend Alison had a few pile ups on her old bike but what is interesting is that what is important for a boy in a crash can be quite different to what is important for a girl.

'I rode my aunt's back pedal bike around the place as a high school girl and also during the six years I had in Canberra. My aunt's bike was green, with no gears. I recall one day when I was about 15 and on my way to school that I sailed past a couple of boys who were in my class who were walking along our regular route to school in a street that ran along-side the local creek. An old timber bridge across the creek had been narrowed to make it a pedestrian only crossing. Just as I was turning to negotiate the white posts blocking cars from going across the bridge, I got swooped by a magpie with the result that I wobbled badly and fell off into a road side tangle of blackberries. Needless to say the immature males from my year coming up behind simply roared with laughter and did nothing to assist me out of the brambles or to reassemble me on my bike.

Then there was the night I was riding up to a friend's house for a party and I got hit by a car that didn't see me in the gloaming of old Canberra's very poor street lighting. Luckily this driver was coming through a give way sign and had slowed down or I might have come to a rather early end. I survived with scrapes on the shins from falling off and the bike was repairable. A white soufflé dish I had in the front carrier was shattered and I had the driver pay up for a new pair of pig skin gloves as they were rather scratched and a shadow of their former elegance.'

Samantha a 26 inch Step Through late 1960's – Sue Thorogood

My wife Sue, like my brother Colin in an earlier chapter, basically talks about the exhilarating feeling that a good bike gives the rider.

'She was big and red and had 26 inch wheels and I didn't have to peddle so fast to cover twice as much ground. My first bike had stabilisers and my little legs went round like crazy as the stabilisers rattled around. Eventually they came off but I still had a small bike, my sister had a Raleigh, I wanted a real bike. Santa brought me Samantha and I loved her, cycling was sheer joy. At one time I had a fold up bike, it wasn't good, I only rode it a few times. It was bought for a holiday in the south of England and almost never used. The holiday was with a girlfriend, Brenda, and we spent more time getting our bikes in and out of the back of the car than we did riding them. After moving to Australia I had a red step through that clanged a lot and was hard to ride, the frame was too small. Tony had a bike with a small frame too so we gave them away. I said I didn't want another bike and wasn't interest in cycling anymore and kept that stance for years but then I found Rosie. She is rosewood in colour, a mixte by Linus Bikes and she is just beautiful. I knew I would like riding her from the moment I sat on the saddle.'

Jane's Semi Racer 1960s/70s – Jane Newbery

Jane was what you would call a Tomboy but actually she was just a girl who liked to enjoy herself and have fun on her bike.

'Used to race my best friend through the main street after school. Two intersections at top racing speed. She never could beat me so gave her head starts but still won. My bike was a semi racer. Ride to top of Black Dump on the "ups and downs", I think this pre dates BMX racing tracks! Took me a while for courage to ride down steep side but I DID. Beat the boys who were too chicken.

Love bike riding but not 100% happy with my bike, I have a new-fangled mountain bike. I miss the old fashioned idea of reverse braking too. And mine has too many gears which stick and confuse me. As my Uncle used to say - you only need 3 gears. Slow Medium and Fast! He used to ride to Adelaide and back in his younger courting days in the 1940's. Ride to Adelaide, buy supplies, go to the dance and court his bride to be - and ride home for work Monday. Trained by riding the 3 towns here

Moonta, Wallaroo, Kadina, 3 times to get a circuit of 100km. Then he knew he was fit enough to get to Adelaide. He lived to a hundred and two.'

Swinging London of the 70's – Susan Tonkin

My friend Susan used to ride one of those small wheeled commuter bikes that were popular at the time and she told me how she had gone to the Adelaide Central Market to do her weekly shop and amongst other things she had bought a bunch of celery which she had tied to the handlebars of her bike. She commenced to cycle home and just up the road from the market a large bus passed her and it got so close that it took the tops off of her celery!

Susan also told me about a play in London.

'I remember seeing a fabulous play in London in the 70s: 'Spokesong' by Stewart Parker. It was a hymn to the bicycle, advocating its wider use in the present day and celebrating its role in changing the lives of previous generations, notably the main character who had been a suffragette. Bicycles for that generation of women did not allow them to get away from the domination of men alas, which continues in all cultures, but it sure got them out of the house. Unless you had a horse (available only to the upper classes) or were a keen walker (strenuous and limiting), the bicycle was practically a woman's only opportunity to get out into the world. Must have been very exciting.'

Dressed to Kill 1970's – Nona Monahin
One way to stop a bike!

'One evening I was riding my bike home from a concert when suddenly it felt like someone had put the brakes on because the bike just wouldn't move, and I almost fell off. I tried to get off the bike but even that was difficult. What had happened was that the edge of my skirt (which was long, and one of those wrap-around skirts that were popular in the seventies) had got into the spokes of the back wheel, which had done several spins before the bike came to a standstill! Meaning the skirt was fairly tightly wound up in the spokes. Took me ages to free it! Imagine standing there, glued to the bike, with half the skirt on me, half inside the wheel… (Good thing it wasn't a scarf around my neck, like poor Isadora Duncan – though she was in a car not a bike).'

The Pushbike Song 1970's – Lisa Maeorg
The Pushbike Song was a hit in England and Australia in the 1970's, there have been a few

pushbike songs and Lisa likes to sing them all as she rides mixing the different songs together.

'I love to ride my bicycle
Turning and turning the wheels go round
Round, round wheels go round and round
Down up pedal, down up down

I sing in my head as I ride my bike. I used to ride lots and lots....I used to ride to school as a student, to teachers college as a student teacher, took my bike to Millicent, my first teaching post, rode in the forests down there, rode to Tantanoola, rode to Robe, bought a new bike when I returned to Adelaide, a blue step through with derailleurs and dropped handlebars, rode from Marryatville to Kingswood and back almost every day when I was teaching there.... Sadly, decided I couldn't ride from Marryatville to Parafield Gardens and back every day, when I worked there, so bought a car....beginning of the end of riding my bike..... But my bike is still here, we yarn bombed it for Tour Down Under this year....'

A Snake in the Grass 1980's – Jenny Statton

I could have written this section, girls on bikes, about the liberating effect of the bicycle on women in the late 1880's and early 1900's, and I have got some of that, but I wanted more than that. I wanted to write about real women riding real bikes and enjoying it and the things that are important to women like earrings and leather gloves and things like that. Jenny, who told me the following stories, certainly enjoyed riding her bike and wore earrings and no lycra.

'One time in Burra, I'm talking about the time I crashed into the bridge near the bowling green, I was on my ten speed bike, the one with dropped handlebars, fiddling with my earring, I'd got the earrings when I went to Queensland, they were beautiful parrots, and one of them fell apart in my hand and I crashed into the bridge, that was a shock.

Another time I was riding on the footpath with Jessica, my daughter, on the back of the bike in a kids seat, I didn't know but she was leaning out and I charged around the corner and bam she hit her head on a fence post. Another time I had a water pipe bike, that's what we called them big and heavy old bikes. It was green, racing green, and I was cycling along the creek on the bike track and there was a brown snake, very poisonous, and I lifted up my legs and went straight over it, scary.

When I was a real little girl I had a dog. Australian Terrier cross with a Fox Terrier, and I had a tricycle but then I got a three wheeler. A tricycle had one big wheel but two little wheels but a three wheeler had three big wheels, I used to say *going to the shops* and my dog would wag his tale and I'd put him in the basket and charge along, my little legs going ten to the dozen and I'd whizz around all over the place. My granddaughter still rides that three wheeler. Once on my three wheeler, I was a little girl in thick glasses with pigtails and I whizzed around the corner of our house and there's a water tank and crash off came the tap then years later Jess, my daughter, was on the same three wheeler, with pigtails and thick glasses and she whizzed around the corner of mum and dad's house and crashed into the water tank and the tap flew off and there was Dad trying to save water with buckets and any container he could find. It was so funny, then he fixed it with rags and concrete, always dripped after that.'

Love on Two Wheels Late 80's – Michelle Christopher

This little tale shows a typical boy showing off and a typical girl not being impressed, bikes can be love machines but not always.

'When I was growing up in Somerset, a boy helped do up my bike in a bid to win my affections. Then he cycled into me and knocked me over. He did a good job on my bike, but knocking me over didn't win him any accolades.'

Tripping 2014 – Ashley from Canberra

Poor old Ashley, bikes are certainly not for her.

'Well I can't ride a bike without it tripping over on rocks or me riding off into a tree or bush, not very fun. Let's just say I prefer to have other transport than bikes.'

Lightweight Frames 2015 – A girl on a bike about men on bikes

This conversation actually happened. I wonder if the lycra clad, carbon fibre fraternity knew what people thought of them, if they would be so eager to show off their excess kilos wrapped in lycra?

'They are obsessed about the weight of the bike but they forget that they are big fat blobs. White lycra is even worse than black and did you know that road racers wee in their pants, they haven't got time to get off the bike and do it. Gross!'

Ros's Grand Tour of Holland 1980 – Ros Barnett
A Tasmanian friend of mine Ros, went on a Grand tour of Holland in September 1980 and her account of that trip makes for a really interesting read.

'I went to live in London early in 1980 with my sweetheart, Scott. He was an accountant and working for one of the big city firms and I had a job as a lab technician in a cramming college.

We bought bicycles for fun, and I used mine to commute. We had chums who had bikes too, so we often rode out into the countryside on Sundays in a small group, seeking out the perfect country pub with a cheap ploughman's lunch and a pint of ale.

Scott and I decided to do our first continental cycling holiday in Holland because it was a soft option. We knew it had first class cycle paths, no or low gradients, and great beer. We were such novice travellers that any way to anywhere would make a pleasant day. We did a bit of research, bought a few maps and train tickets to Oostende and away we went. It was September 1980.

Really that was all we needed; bikes and a map. Our first adventure was exploring Oostende. We ate moules and drank beer on the docks, and then had a little sleep on the beach. We decided to ride the 10km to Brugge to spend our first night since it was a pretty town with lots of tourist accommodation. I still remember that ride as one of the best of my life. The bike path followed a canal, with fields and windmills and quaint bridges, and other cyclists waved happy greetings. The world seemed a very perfect place.

To my Australian eyes Brugge was almost magical. We found a brilliant little guest house where they were happy to look after our bikes and we wandered around the town, mesmerised. I discovered a little shop that sold the most divine little hazelnut chocolates shaped like seashells. You see them everywhere these days but that was my very first time and I thought I had died and gone to heaven.

After Brugge we visited Ghent and Antwerp but decided we preferred the smaller villages so for the next few days we wandered around the countryside with our only plan to head in the general direction of Nijmegen where one of my university lecturers was living.

With a little inside knowledge gleaned from my friend in Nijmegen we made next for the Hoge Veluwe National Park. The attraction for us was the Kroller-Muller Museum where I was going to see my very first Van Gogh up close and personal, along with the odd Picasso and Mondrian. That day was another that I remember as a day of sensory overload. The landscape of the park, with deer and wild pigs crossing the paths in front of us, and sand dunes mixed with pine forests, and no cars at all, didn't prepare us for the dramatic modern architecture of the museum and the stunning art collection. Much of the building is underground and we wandered for hours just stunned.

I remember we stayed until closing time and then had to be urged toward the exit. We found our bikes were getting lonely in the bike rack, and the sun was getting low in the sky. My legs felt like lead. It was only a few kilometres to the park boundary and we decided that we would stop at the very first 'zimmer frei' that we came to, but it happened that we had to ride all the way to Nijkerke, probably 15 kilometres before we found a place where we could get a meal and a bed. It was an ugly roadhouse that we might normally have passed by, but it taught us a lesson. It was clean and comfortable, the food was brilliant, and it was cheap. But best of all, the thing the trip had been missing to that point, was that it was full of Dutch people and they embraced us. We had a lot of beer and sang songs and laughed until the wee small hours of the morning.

The next morning our new best friends insisted we have an uitsmijter breakfast, to ease our hangovers, and we loved it so much we had one almost every day thereafter. An uitsmijter is bread and ham and eggs done in a particular Dutch style, and more than once we washed it down with Belgian lager.

Our bikes were both Peugeot, with Reynolds 531 tubing and shimano gear. They were touring bikes, not top of the range by any means but not cheap either, and we were very fond of them so when they were stolen from outside our Amsterdam hotel we were devastated. We had only just checked in and put our luggage in our room and were just about to go out to the street where the bikes were locked to a railing and move them to a yard off a lane at the back when a young girl came in to tell us that she had just seen two men in a van pull up, cut the locks off the bikes, and drive away with them. She was visiting her grandmother next door and witnessed all this from the window. She had already phoned the police and given them a description and the van's number plate.'

Unfortunately for Ros and Scott their bikes were never recovered but they bought new bikes in Holland from the insurance money and kept cycling.

Part Seven
Bicycle Touring

Ramsgate to Lands End
Part One: London to Ramsgate and Back
I remember the trip vividly, I had my brand new Revell touring bike, it was silver grey with red handle bar tape. I was rearing to go, even though I had to travel with my injured right hand from my accident in Greenwich. The first day involved cycling one handed through the busy metropolis and out into the Surrey countryside. I went on a major arterial road to the south of London, there were lovely old English homes but far too many cars so I got onto the back roads and cycled down a sunken lane where the road, over the centuries, had been worn away by traffic. Up above me the trees either side formed an honour guard, it was incredibly beautiful. I cycled on and suddenly came to an Olde Worlde England of Agatha Christie's Miss Marple, of picture postcard villages, thatched cottages set around village greens, duck ponds, babbling brooks and fields surrounded by high hedgerows, there was even village cricket being played. I picked blackberries from the hedgerows and had to dismount at one stage as a most lethal looking farm

machine came along a tiny country lane and my bike and I had to push ourselves into the hedge not to be chopped and trampled to death.

My first stop was Canterbury where I spent time exploring the cathedral, in all the world Canterbury cathedral is my favourite, then I was off again. I rode through a diminutive village called Monkton and then another called Minster and found myself in the bungalow paradise of outer Ramsgate where my favourite Aunty lived.

After staying a couple of days with Aunty Laura I cycled to a Roman ruin, Richborough, then on to a quaint village called Sandwich with its barbican, old gateway, and half-timbered houses, it was very pretty. Next was the seaside town of Deal with its pebble beach and white Georgian guest houses piled up like unkempt grenadier guards and a coastal defensive fort built to frustrate Napoleon's idea of invading England, it consisted of a series of interlocking circles, quite impressive really.

As I rode along the south coast of England one thing I noticed was the wind. It came at me from all directions, I didn't seem to be able to get away from it, even inland it seemed windy but I just geared down a bit and kept on pedalling. Years later when cycling in Burra my wife Sue complained that no matter which direction we cycled in we always seemed to have a head wind.

Dover along the coast had its impressive castle and its spectacular white cliffs and I climbed up to the old Norman castle, there is also a Roman lighthouse there. I found Dover a bit big, a bit busy and a bit depressing, so I made my way to Folkestone and had fish and chips on the front. Mostly the cycling was easy as I was near the coast, there were the North Downs to contend with, chalk hills that created the white cliffs of Dover, but there were not so many hills to go up. After Hythe I went by the Dymchurch Redoubt, another anti Napoleonic fortress, also used in World War Two in case Hitler's Nazis got across the English Channel, and I came to Dymchurch where I cycled along the front. Both Dymchurch and Hythe were well stocked with Martello towers, gun turrets, set up along the coast to repel Napoleon's invasion of England, so really I was cycling along the anti-Napoleon coast. Eventually I came to the Cinque Port of Romney. I'd never heard the term before and still can't pronounce it, but Cinque Ports, such as Romney, are ancient defensive towns built to stop invasion from the sea by Vikings and that sort of thing. It was a well defended coast but they didn't stop William the Conqueror!

Hastings was another seaside town with white encrustations along its front. I found some fishermen's huts for drying nets that I remembered from when I had been in Hastings as a boy, about twenty years before! They were like black coffins standing on end. Then I was off again. I cycled past a bit of a hill called Battle where the battle of Hastings had been fought, poor old King Harold was hacked to death there defending England against the Normans. I was in the Weald of Kent or is it the Weald of Sussex? The Weald is an ancient forest, to the north and south of the Weald are the North and South Downs and, although they are called Downs, the word means up, they are wooded gently rolling hills and somewhere in there I stumbled on two cyclists Cath, with buffy blonde hair, and Carole, a bit thinner with straight blonde hair. They had stopped and were talking about how beautiful the Downs were, or was it how beautiful the Weald was, or was it the ups? Anyway I stopped too.

Cath rode her dad's light blue ten speed bike and Carole her mum's light pink ten speed, they were just tootling around cycling in the South Downs for a few days, we got talking and the upshot of that was that we cycled off into the Weald together. We passed a local folly, it was a tall structure put up by a farmer years before in Brightling East Sussex, the girls called it Farmer Jack Fuller's Folly or the Brightling Needle. The next day we went into Royal Tunbridge Wells and bought striped T-Shirts at a sale. Mine consisted of great bands of brown and white picked out by narrow bands of red, it was fairly tight fitting and I was very slim and I did look good even if I say so myself. We three in our new T-shirts certainly looked a lot nicer than the modern cyclist in their ugly lycra. The next day, after a sojourn in a Youth Hostel, we rode on passing an old water mill and went by a movie being filmed on location about witches and the girls, but not me, saw naked women frolicking in a haystack. We shot along country lanes and went through endless picture postcard villages and eventually came to a busy town which had posh suburban houses with big gardens. We had formed a team, cycling lazily through the English countryside, but now it was over. The girls stopped, Cath spoke to Carole, they came over to me and gave me big kisses and then rode north into London.

I kept going into Surrey and met ever heavier traffic, well actually very heavy traffic, I can still see the cars and trucks. There was a cutting in the hillside, the road was wide, two lanes each way, and there were trucks and fumes and it felt very busy and fast and dangerous. I was going uphill, I geared down and was hit by diesel fumes so I turned off into some back streets, got lost and then found my way to Walton on Thames.

Part Two: Swanage Here I Come
After a couple of days with friends in London I was off on my deadly treadly. I cycled through some affluent outer suburbs with big houses, neo-Tudor in architecture, with big gardens, one garden had a miniature steam train going around and around in it! I rode along a country lane on a ridge, the countryside dropped away on either side and the view was just beautiful. Down in a valley was the village of Normandy, apparently the name has nothing to do with Normandy in France but is a corruption of Nobodies Common, the common land there was owned by two villages so nobody actually owned it. I looked down, saw it lying there asking

me to come and explore but I resisted temptation and cycled on to Aldershot and Farnham. The traffic was horrific all busy, busy going somewhere or doing something, I abandoned busy roads for country lanes and came to a lovely quaint old village, Old Alresford, and on to the Georgian New Alresford with a quaint row of shops. I passed a water meadow where watercress was growing in a babbling brook, got off my bike, walked onto an old bridge and just gazed down it looked so quintessentially English.

A quick sprint down the road was Winchester of Winchester Cathedral fame. I looked at the Cathedral and the Statue of King Arthur, or was it a statue of King Alfred who burnt the cakes? It seemed like a nice town but I didn't hang around instead I took a convoluted route along the back lanes. I tried to follow an old Roman road and I also tried to catch sight of the Iron Age Hill Fort of Danebury but I didn't have time to stop as I wanted to get to see Stonehenge, one of the greatest prehistoric monuments in the world, before nightfall.

At Stonehenge I pedalled by hundreds of tourists disembarking from their tour buses and heading to the old pile of masonry so I gave Stonehenge the big miss and turned towards the cathedral town of Salisbury. It was getting late so I took a short cut along a country road, the country road turned into a country lane, the country lane turned into a farm track and the farm track turned into a field. I had nowhere to go so I turned around and cycled back the way I had come. I was now back on a main road and I had a slow puncture in my back tyre, it was very annoying. I was cold and tired after my long diversion and I had to keep stopping to pump up my tyre. The sun had set, there was still a little twilight but only a very little and the traffic kept thundering by.

I had some new-fangled French lights which I carried in my saddlebag, they attached quickly when one needed them. I needed them so I stopped, attached them, pumped up my tyre and continued to bump along for a while then I stopped and pumped up my back tyre some more. A column of tanks came out of the darkness and charged at me, I was on Salisbury Plain a vast area run by the British Army and criss-crossed by public roads. There I was a cyclist with ineffectual lights, a flat back tyre and army tanks with very ineffectual vision speeding passed me in the dark. One nudge from any of those monsters and I would be dead. Thankfully I wasn't nudged, I lived and limped in the dark into Salisbury.

My puncture fixed, next morning I was up bright and early and charged down the hill I had walked my lame bike up the night before. An English Bobby, a policeman, standing at the bottom of the hill called me over, he said he was going to book me for speeding, I told him, in the broadest Australian accent I could muster, that I was flying back to Australia in a couple of days so he let me off.

I explored the cathedral in Salisbury, it's quite spectacular, big spire, lovely grounds and a really good bookshop in the cathedral close. Further on I discovered an interesting Roman villa in the back blocks, Rockbourne Roman Villa and I kept peddling until I came to a typical thatched cottage country pub. I stopped and had a pint of real ale and a ploughman's lunch which consisted of a hunk of bread, a chunk of cheddar cheese, some pickle and a pickled onion.

My cycle marathon, or should that be cyclethon, then took me to the New Forest, a game park set aside by William the Conqueror (1066 and all that) for him and his mates, the Norman knights, to romp around the countryside hunting. The first thing that happened to me in the New Forest was a wild pig ran across the road in front of my wheels, I had to use my breaks pretty sharply to avoid a collision with half a ton of bacon. I found the Rufus Stone where William the Conqueror's son died, shot with an arrow, and I also found a World War Two airbase at Stoney Cross. The runways were still there and I cycled up and down the same runways used by US Air Force bombers and Royal Air Force Hurricane fighters to take off to fight the Luftwaffe in World War Two.

As evening drew in I pushed along the main arterial roads of the New Forest into Christchurch, that looked interesting but daylight was running out so I rode on into some rather depressing major intersections joining lots of arterial roads. I didn't want to be there so I cycled faster and found myself in the Victorian seaside town of Bournemouth. There was a pier and a cobbled beach and I rode past chines, hollow ways in the cliffs that led down to the beach. Time was moving on and I had to get to the youth hostel in Swanage so I raced along Sandbanks, a great sand dune cutting off Poole Harbour which is supposedly the same size as

Sydney harbour, Sandbanks was chock-a-block with seaside mansions of various millionaires. The road was flat and I really picked up some speed, then I came to the ferry that serviced the harbour, it was quaint and old worldly, nice to see. On the other side I remounted, pushed off and raced past a nature park in the dunes, the park was full of heather in full bloom and as the sun set the purple lavender coloured flowers of the heather were just stunning, I have never seen heather like that again.

I charged on, around and over and up and down twisting country lanes with very high hedges, it was pitch black, I couldn't see a thing. I was worried that other vehicles wouldn't see me as, for some reason, perhaps I was in a hurry, I didn't put my lights on. Luckily I wasn't hit by anything and I was soon speeding through Swanage. I rode past the tourist beach, the hotels and the bed and breakfasts, through the shopping street, past the fish and chip shop and a pub called The Swan, or something like that, and then up a very steep hill. My bike could handle any hill but that hill in Swanage, up to the Youth Hostel, is a doozy, I checked in, went to my room and lay down, I was tired.

That night I sat on the front porch of the Youth Hostel with an Australian girl who worked there. We talked, I told her I was looking for work she said that I could have her job as she was going back to Australia in a week. She said, *Ring up in seven days and I will have fixed it with the boss.*

Part Three: Swanage to Lands End and Back
Next morning I was up bright and early, mounted my bike and sped along country lanes past a castle at the junction of two ridges, Corfe Castle, a picture postcard castle with a picture postcard village but I had no time to stop I was on my way to Land's End.

To get there I passed through Dorchester and on to see the Cerne Abbass Giant with his big stick and great big phallus. From Dorchester it was on to Loders and Uploders, I visited those two villages just for their names, and then to Bridport, famous for making rope. Working my way through the ups and downs of the countryside I got to Lyme Regis, locked up my bike and walked out onto the famous causeway, The Cobb, a stone breakwater that juts out into the sea and made famous in Jane Austen's *Persuasion* and the movie *The French Lieutenant's Woman*. The French Lieutenant's Woman, as I recall, consisted of the heroine sitting on the end of The Cobb in stormy seas.

Lyme Regis done I was back on the steep country lanes in the back blocks and charged on to a town called Beer where I booked into the Youth Hostel and went to the pub with a couple of fellow cyclists. They talked gear ratios and derailleurs and wanted to know all about mine as I had passed them with such ease earlier in the day. I didn't have too much technical jargon to give them I just said, *My bike has a brilliant set of gears and these,* and I slapped my thigh muscles. I had thigh muscles like iron.

One of the secrets of my ease when cycling through the English countryside was that I travelled light. I had two pannier bags for the trip but left one in London and cycled with the other one, it contained a pair of sandals, a spare pair of undies, a spare T-shirt, soap and tooth brush, a towel, a sheet, a tool kit and a good map, oh yes and a novel, but not a thick novel, and my trusty Swiss Army knife. I also dressed sensibly. I wore shorts, no lycra and no cycling shoes, a red University of Adelaide T-shirt and a light pair of docksider sailing shoes. Having a very light load meant that the hills that killed other cyclists were just a little bit of a push for me and life on the road was all pleasure. Simple dress and almost no baggage made me very efficient and fast.

Next day I was off again, this time to Sidmouth. I was on a back lane hurtling down a hill with a tight right angled turn and the sea in front, I looked over my shoulder and saw a field full of donkeys all staring at me. It was the Donkey Sanctuary of Elizabeth Svendsen fame. In Sidmouth it was drizzling, a sort of stinging cold rain, and a gust of wind tried to pick me and my bike up and throw us down, I got off and walked along the front pushing my bike against the howling wind. A lady rugged up from head to foot came up to me and said that she much preferred this weather to the real hot summer days when it got to 25°C! *Where I come from 40°C is common in summer,'* I said and she shuddered. The intrepid cyclist, that's me, cycled on, past Axminster, where they make the famous carpet and then Exmouth, I can still see a vision of the estuary with sailing boats and barges and some Dutch style houses. I carried on into Exeter where I had a quick look around, it looked nice, there was a green in the centre of town and yet another beautiful cathedral, I didn't go in the cathedral. How many cathedrals does a person need to visit? Then I was off to Dartmoor.

Dartmoor was the first real goal of my trip, I wanted to see the stone age round houses and the clapper bridges. As I cycled across the moor the light was just beginning to fade, it was misty and a light drizzle was falling, it was very atmospheric. I passed a famous tor, an outcrop of rocks, it was quite stark and sculpturesque and then I pulled on the brakes, stood my bike up against a ruined dry stone wall and tracked down a muddy path to the old stone age round houses I had been dreaming of. The houses were still outlined in stone for all the world to see, an original stone age village, brilliant. I trekked back to my bike and sped down the hill to the youth hostel at Two Bridges in the mist and drizzle.

The next day the sun was shining, it was a beautiful morning, the water was trickling through peat in the local babbling brook and I walked over and inspected the two bridges. One was an old stone road bridge and the other, the clapper bridge, was built in medieval times for donkeys and mules to cross with copper or wheat or wool or the mail or whatever on their backs. Clapper bridges on Dartmoor consist of great slabs of stone placed on great stone buttresses, very simple and very lovely.

Then I was back on my bike again racing across the moor, actually it was a slow cycle up hill and then a sprint downhill into Tavistock. The moor was beautiful, more open country than you get almost anywhere in England, the colours were brilliant, there was the purple of the heather and rich browns and oranges of the scrub and the green of the grass and moss but a more subdued green than the usual bright green of England.

On my tour I didn't worry too much about food, in Cornwall and Devon I ate the famous dish of the region, tea, scones, jam, made from local fruit, and clotted cream. I cycled in the mornings until about 10am then I would keep my eyes open for a farmhouse that had a sign stating, AFTERNOON TEA, I'd dismount, lean my bike against a hedge or dry stone wall, lock it and then humbly ask the farmer's wife, *It's not too early for afternoon tea is it?* Often they said it was but just as often I scored afternoon tea. I ate it in farmhouses, in shops in seaport towns like Fowey and on seaside piers jutting into the sea and once, while crossing Exmoor, I managed to get some in an old farmhouse where the clotted cream had just been made by an eighty year old lady and the scones were fresh out of the oven, heaven! I think it was the clotted cream,

I just loved the stuff, I ladled it on. I didn't think about lunch, I cycled on until it was really time for afternoon tea and then I would find a tea shop or farmhouse for tea, scones jam and clotted cream once again.

After Tavistock I headed to the coast. The coast there was all hills and dips, valleys and cliffs, absolutely stunning countryside, with England at its most verdant and the grey blue sea crashing ashore under white cliffs and of course seaside resorts and fishing villages. I went through Polperro to Fowey where I caught a ferry and then on to St Austell where I had afternoon tea in a tea shop with big old fashioned bay windows in the high street. That night I went through a village called Gweek and came to the Youth Hostel at Coverack. All the talk at the Youth Hostel was the Lizard this and the Lizard that, the Lizard is a peninsula that juts out into the sea, I didn't go down to the Lizard, the youth hostel at Coverack is set up on the hillside and had a mega view of the little harbour and boats out to sea and headlands, I just sat and watched and drank tea and ate scones with clotted cream.

The next day I was off to Penzance, famous for the Gilbert and Sullivan operetta *The Pirates of the said*

Penzance. First I rode to St Michael's Mount, an old monastery on a rock in the sea, when the tide comes in the old monastery is cut off. I walked across the causeway and mooched about a bit, I had the place to myself, which is unusual in England, then I returned to my intrepid bike. At Penzance I stayed a few days walking to Mousehole, pronounced moos-ole. I had a drink in the pub and then a group of us walked around the cliff tops to the Minack Theatre, an old Greek theatre look alike built on the cliffs. We watched a Greek tragedy, Oedipus Rex or the Bacchae or something, the setting was wonderful, the acoustics were great, the only problem was that the sea crashed on the rocks at the bottom of the theatre and that sounded great too, possibly too great.

The following day I rode around the foot of England to Land's End, walked through a sort of souvenir shop and got to the very end of England. I walked around the cliffs, the waves were crashing and it was pretty stunning, I had reached my goal, *I can die now,* I thought. No I didn't, what I did was get back on my bike and ride to Saint Just, an old stone built copper mining town, and then around the somewhat desolate peninsula past many old mining towers to the tourist beach of St Ives which was very pleasant, very pleasant indeed. It straddles its own bay like a man tucking his arm around his lover and it was full of holidaymakers and holidaymakers' knick-knack shops.

One of the joys of cycling in Cornwall and Devon was the ferries I had to use to get over the many streams and rivers. At one stage I lifted my bike onto my shoulder and hiked across the sand to a pedestrian ferry, boarded, was taken across the river and then landed on the beach and carried my bike back up and onto the road.

As arranged I rang Swanage youth hostel from Penzance, they told me I had a job and just one week to cycle all the way back. So I took off, quick sharp, and peddled up the north coast of Cornwall, past the surfing beach of Newquay, to me it looked a bit cold for surfing, having had my irrelevant thought I cycled on to the ruined King Arthurian Castle of Tintagel. I rode along the cliff tops and got to a beautiful old Cornish cottage just on the edge of the cliffs, the youth hostel. The next day I explored the castle, it is a rocky, romantic, rugged and beautiful place.

Having given Tintagel the once over I rode on to the famous Cornish fishing village of Clovelly, a beautiful spot with its lovely little harbour at the bottom. It had no cars, just donkeys, because the road was so steep, it is even hard to walk down. I got off my bike and tried to walk my bike down the road but it was too difficult so I got back on and rode down the hill instead with the breaks on full, that was easier. Then I rode to Barnstaple and on to Exmoor which was my goal that day. I found Exmoor more tame than Dartmoor but in a small village up there on the moor I had the most memorable afternoon tea, then I cycled on into Somerset through the Quantock Hills and on to Glastonbury, King Arthurs old capital, which was the famous Island of Avalon and has quite an impressive old monastery or the ruin thereof. There was also a very impressive chapel on top of a great mound in otherwise totally flat country, I guess that was the Somerset Levels. At one stage during the day I found a bike shop in Taunton and purchased a pile of spokes and in the evening I came to Street where the youth hostel was and I booked a bed.

I got to talking to people at Street youth hostel, as one does, and they wanted me to come down to the pub with them but I couldn't, first I had to turn my bike upside down, quick release the back wheel, strip off the tyre, the tube and the cloth lining and rebuild the thing. My bike was a beauty, light weight with a good feel and it could get me up any hill with ease but it had an Achilles Heel, the spokes in the back wheel kept going ping. That day up in the hills I had so many pings I had to stop and do emergency repairs on the side of the road. I would disassemble the wheel, take some spokes from one side and place them on the other to try and balance up the gismo. I ran out of spare spokes! As part of my kit I carried a spoke key, half a dozen spokes and a file. I rebuilt the wheel, sometimes up to once every day, then spun it and adjusted it to get it back into alignment. I got quite good at building wheels.

The next day was Somerset. I remember a particularly challenging hill on the road south approaching Dorchester then it was back on the road I had travelled two weeks earlier and there was the picture postcard Corfe Castle, Corfe village and then around the Purbeck range into Swanage where I was to work.

Part Eight
Long Distance

Crossing the Nullarbor

In Australia, crossing the Nullarbor Plain is considered a cycling feat to be proud of. The Nullarbor stretches from outback South Australia right across The Great Australian Bight and to the Gold Fields in Western Australia. The word Nullarbor is actually Latin, it means no trees but in fact lots of shrubs and bushes grow there and there are very famous underground caves. Also the Nullarbor is a great place for whale watching. Its drawback is it's hot, dusty, fly blown and no body lives there. There are however lots of road houses as it's crossed by the interstate highway between Sydney, Adelaide and Perth. It's also crossed by the famous Indian Pacific Railway.

My friend Andy, Andrea, wrote to me about the Nullarbor she said: 'Cathy's dad did it. He rode alone from Adelaide to Perth. My friend Sarah lives in Western Australia she did it west to east with three friends. She grew bean sprouts in a jar tied to her handlebars. Back then you needed to post food packages to key places along the way. Not much fresh food to be had.'

Garret and Clea, a couple from Sydney, rode a Cannondale tandem across the Nullarbor setting off in March 2009 from Sydney and arriving in Perth 32 days and 3695 kilometres later. See Clea's blog cyclenullabor.wordpress.com. On the first day they got up at 4am to get through Sydney before the place was overrun with traffic. Clea writes: 'To our surprise a bunch of our buddies were waiting outside our gate to send us off and even rode with us the whole way into Sydney and helped us get the tandem up the Harbour Bridge steps.'

The first day was a hard slog and there were lots more hard slogs to come as they cycled through The Great Dividing Range. Finally they got to Moss Vale pitched their tent and then a massive rain storm soaked them, their gear and their tent. They hired a caravan and were in bed at 6.30pm. The next day they cycled to Yass and Clea wrote: 'I could barely walk and the motion of going sitting to standing was painful.'

Day five and things like peddling the bike became easier and the traffic started to disappear from the road. Day six was going to be hot so they set off early catching a beautiful sunrise plus the native wildlife. 'We past a huge eagle just a stone's throw from the road just as it took flight.' Day seven she wrote, 'flying along on a bike with no trucks, cars, traffic lights or hills.' Hills were one of their unexpected problems so called flat Australia seemed to have a lot of hills. Mosquitoes were another problem as was a sore bum until Garrett bought a new saddle.'

Day eight: 'Here's a word for the unwise. Never ride a bike from Balranald to Mildura when it is 37°C.' They rode through the day and found that there was no shade and no place to escape from the endless heat. The heat in the Australian Outback can drive you mad and even kill you.

The Nullarbor was, 'Flat, flat flat and nothing, nothing, nothing.' They pulled into a clifftop viewpoint on the Great Australian Bight and Clea wrote: 'The cliffs on the Bight are breathtaking, so high and treacherous looking, and the vista goes on and on.' And on the Nullarbor they even spotted a rare black dingo. A dingo is an Australian wild dog.

Just ten kilometres after a place with a typically Western Australian name Mundrabilla, no it was after Mundrabilla, at Madura disaster struck. They heard a strange noise and the rim on the back wheel of the tandem had cracked. They rode on, what else can you do out in the Australian bush, then they came across caravaners Shirley and Scott who pushed the tandem into their caravan and gave Garrett and Clea a four hundred Kilometre lift to Norseman. At Norseman Garrett got onto the phone and the bike people at Cannondale, the tandem was a Cannondale, put a new back wheel on a truck to be delivered to them.

Eventually the truck with the new wheel arrived, Garrett replaced the broken wheel and it was on to Widgiemooltha where one of the world's largest chunks of gold was found, not unfortunately by Garrett and Clea . 'The road around there felt hazardous,' Clea wrote, 'loads of trucks, no shoulder and heaps of blind corners.' They were fast approaching civilisation. Last day: 'We made it to Mundaring, 30k out of Perth, by lunchtime and from there it was all downhill, top speed 65k per hour.' Cycling through the city was terrifying after four weeks of little traffic and no traffic lights but they made it. In Clea's words: 'Garrett and I felt tired and sore but very happy as we cycled the last tiny bit into Subiaco where a nice cup of tea and a properly cooked hot meal were waiting.'

I asked Garrett about the tandem he and Clea crossed the Nullarbor on: 'The bike was a 2004 Canondale road tandem, ten speed with disc brakes. We had a bob trailer to carry the camping gear and added extra water bottles.

I chose a tandem as I planned to do the ride solo thinking there was zero chance my partner wanted to go. Upon discovering my plans she said that she wanted to tackle the challenge. I know there was no way we could do it on two bikes and stay together as I had been a semi-professional cyclist with the Canadian National Team and she was an office worker who occasionally cycled. So I thought a tandem.

'The bike went well due to a lot of obsessing over details and upgrades. There was only one part that I didn't get the chance to upgrade and that was the part that let us down. The rear wheel exploding just outside of Cockalbiddy in Western Australia. I contacted Cannondale in Perth and they had my exact same bike on the showroom floor. The rep took the rear wheel off and put it onto a refrigeration truck crossing the Nullarbor and the wheel arrived in Norseman after a three day wait.

'A couple of interesting statistics: at the beginning of our ride across Australia I weighted 84kg and Clea 72kg by the end I weighted 75KG and Clea 69kg. We reached our top speed of the trip coming over the top in the Flinders Ranges at 75 kilometres an hour.'

I spoke to Garrett about his early career in cycle racing. 'I was a junior cross country champion in my area of the West Coast of British Colombia. When I moved to the big smoke I started racing criterium road bikes at the university to make extra cash for food and rent.' A criterium, is a bike race consisting of several laps around a closed circuit. 'Eventually I was selected to represent Canada in the World Championships. I also competed in the local mountain bike races in Vancouver. I secured a few sponsors and that helped with entry fees, clothing and food while racing. Things were going well for me then I broke my spine in three places while competing. It took me nearly two years to recover. You may think it was time for me to give cycling away but with rehab and a lot of hard work I was back. After moving to Australia I carried on with free riding and ultra-endurance and even dabbled in mountain bike racing as a way to see my new country.'

A Bicycle Made for Five

Andrew an environmentalist who's working here in Ross is a keen cyclist, when I asked him how many bikes he owns he said something like fifteen later he clarified that statement fifteen in his immediate family. One of his bikes is a five seater. It was originally made by a crazy guy who knocked up bikes for the Norwood Christmas Pageant, in Adelaide, for clowns to ride. The crazy guy even made bikes with egg shaped wheels and bikes that were double height.

Over a cup of tea Andrew told me that he and a friend rode the five seater to the Adelaide Grand Prix car race. The bike was covered in anti-Grand Prix slogans, anti-car slogans and 'stuff like how people die doing stupid things in cars.' Their plan was to get onto the track at the Grand Prix and cycle round before the race began. They nearly managed it but at the last moment security cottoned on to them. They decided to cycle off home and a waysider shouted; 'give us a lift.' They stopped established that they were in fact going in the same direction and they gave the fella a lift. In gratitude their ride bought them a slab of beer, that's Australian for a carton of beer.

Another time Andrew was contemplating riding from Adelaide to Cairns in Queensland about five thousand kilometres and his dad said to him: 'You'll never make it,' that spurned him on so he set off with a mate camping rough every night and only paying for accommodation once and that was a mere dollar. It took Andrew nine months to get to Cairns but that involved only fifty days of cycling. He worked from time to time on the journey and on one occasion he house sat for a month for some people going off to see the Flying Yogi.

While cycling through Victoria he and his mate went to a rock concert, they locked their bikes in a car. Andrew gave the key to his mate and said: 'Whatever you do don't lose it.' After a weekend of sex & drugs & rock & roll Andrew's friend had lost everything he owned including the key. So they drove the car to the local town outside the local cop shop there was a man with an angel grinder, 'can you cut this lock off for us?' they said and he did.

On one occasion Andrew was cycling along, he'd split up with his mate by now, he came across a woman cycling with a dog in a trailer. She was riding all the way to Darwin for some charity or other and Andrew took pity on her and toed the trailer for a day.

The cycle through Queensland Sugar Cane Country was pivotal to Andrews development as a human being. It was hot and there were no trees and he decided then and there that the world needed more shade, more trees. After he reached Cairns he went back to Adelaide and studied environmental management. Since then one of Andrew's biggest projects was to help organise the planting of five million trees.

I was talking to Andrew recently and he had just been riding some of the trails at the Derby Mountain Bike Track in North Eastern Tasmania, as he flew down a particularly steep track he started saying to himself 'I'm forty something years old what am I doing here?'

Training and Racing Bicycles
Nigel Davies a super keen racing cyclist here in Ross rides a very much all singing and dancing

carbon fibre super bike he bought in Germany and had air freighted to Australia. He wrote the following article: **Training and Racing Bicycles** about artificial intelligence in cycling.

'I'm seventy five years old and recently won my age group in the Australian Gran Fondo Championship. This article describes the race and how I used computer software to generate a training plan for the event.

Gran Fondos, or 'big rides' to use the English translation, are endurance rides of anywhere from 50 – 250 kilometres patronised by hundreds or thousands of cyclists. The Australian Championships course, in Perth, West Australia, was six laps of a 13.6 km circuit with a couple of climbs each lap – total distance 83 km and total climb 1,158 metres.

The art of training for a bike race is to take the number of hours available for cycling each week and devise the optimum mix of short rides and long rides, easy rides and intense, hard rides to achieve the best possible result on race day.

Artificial intelligence (AI) has now arrived in bike racing in the form of a program called Xert. You enter the date, distance and metres climbed of the race, your target race finishing time, the number of hours you are prepared to train per week, your current level of fitness, and the software will either say "not achievable" or generate a training program to achieve the desired performance level by race day.

I typed in the race distance and climb, with a target finish time of 2 hours and 40 minutes and available training time per week of 10 hours. I downloaded my last ten years of digital training records into the software so the AI could get to work on a forecast.

The first win was that the software said that the target finish time was achievable, and it generated a training program based on my available hours and days of the week. Each day, in the four months leading up to the event, I was asked to ride a certain number of kilometres at a specified speed – or to do nothing for the day and rest and recover.
Come race day my fitness had improved by 19% - from 217 watts to 258 watts, to use the arcane functional threshold power, or FTP, that cyclists use to measure performance. I travelled to Perth with

my bike, registered for the race the day before, and lined up at the start with all the other competitors.

The race was six laps around King's Park in central Perth, with a section along the banks of the Swan River and up through the city before looping back into the park. We set off at a cracking pace and I found myself riding with a bunch of younger competitors. In a race it is much easier to ride behind other people, or 'draughting' as it's called, rather than riding solo and having to overcome the wind resistance independently. I stuck with this bunch and put in sufficient effort on the hills each lap to keep pace with them.

Two hours and 21 minutes later I passed the finish line in first place for my age group with an average speed of 34.2 km/hr and 19 minutes faster than the original target time.

The most interesting thing about the training was that the 'hard' days were so much more demanding than anything I had done previously. For example, I used to think that three by five-minute maximum intensity efforts was adequate for a hard day, but by the end of the program I was doing twelve by five-minute efforts, with five minutes of recovery between each one. This was designed to correspond to the six-lap race with two by five-minute climbs each lap.

I really like how the software took the guesswork out of training. Once you learn to trust the system, you go out on a training day, download the requirements to the bike computer and ride until you complete them. I learned two things from this: previously, my hard training days weren't hard enough, and my 'easy' training days were too easy, which is a bit surprising as you usually read that people do their easy days too hard. On easy days I used to cruise around at an easy pace for 3 – 4 hours and enjoy the day. The easy day program required two or three 20-minute efforts at a higher pace, which made the easy days much more challenging.

What's next? Well, the World Gran Fondo Championships will be held in Australia next October. I have already put in a new and more ambitious target time to the Xert software. It says it is achievable, but I will have to be prepared to train for up to 15 hours a week to make it. We'll see how it goes! Nigel Davies, 16 May 2025

Stop Press: Nigel sprinted home to wine by one second.

LEJOG & JOGLE.

LEJOG refers to the long-distance cycle route from Land's End in England to John o' Groats in Scotland, spanning the length of mainland Britain. Some people ride it in reverse: JOGLE.

The route for the LEJOG takes in old railways now paved, bridleways, footpaths and toe paths along the many British canals but it sounds easier than it is. In one blog I read the author stated: 'The downside to avoiding the main roads of course is that the smaller country roads are hillier. The path got very narrow in places with my legs brushing past over-growing nettles, I was only wearing shorts I wasn't best pleased. Later on the track I should have taken was underwater.'

In Scotland the anonymous blogger had a rather interesting experience: 'I was cycling too fast when suddenly I came across a very muddy stretch four to five metres long. I entered the mud too fast and found myself battling hard with the bike to stay upright. I stayed in control and made it out of the mud with my heart beating fast.'

The above mentioned blogger had a plethora of mechanical failures, spokes breaking in Cornwall, in northern England one of his pedals sheared off and in Scotland his rear wheel cracked and had to be replaced. Having replaced his rear wheel he set off happily only to find that his rear tyre had split and needed replacing. Later as he approached John o' Groats his rear brake completely packed in. I think he must have been jinxed.

Eventually he got to John o' Groats: 'It was a bit surreal really weeks and weeks of cycling and the destination was finally in sight! A long descent into the harbour and it was over. I'd dreamt about the moment for the whole ride, the sense of satisfaction and pride has been great.'

Highland Fling
It was in the early 1980's when I got up early one morning and toured the old Viking town of York in northern England walking around the walls, visiting the Minster and an incredible medieval street full of butcher's shops, called The Shambles. I'd left my towel in the Youth Hostel where I was staying the night before so I found a cheap shop and bought a cheap towel. I wanted a cheap towel as they are thin and dry quickly very important when life is a series of one night stands. I mounted my Revell ten speed touring bike that I'd bought in Hampstead, London

and started what I thought would be a leisurely cruise across The Yorkshire Dales to the Lake District. The ride started off as an easy pedal. I remember cycling through Knaresborough alongside the castle, blown up by Oliver Cromwell's Round Heads, and across the bridge and thinking I wish I had time for a look around. Then I was cycling through Harrogate with its Stray, an area of extensive lawns dotted on that day by crocuses they looked very beautiful.

I cycled north to Ripon and there was an interesting looking Cathedral but I was starting to run out of time so I put on a burst of speed and got to Leyburn, another interesting spot, but I was definitely running late. I charged through James Herriot's country, James Herriot famous for the television show All Creatures Great and Small was a vet in the Yorkshire Dales. I got to Hawes and the day was starting to come to an end. I remember Hawes distinctly, there was a railway viaduct somewhere there and it all seemed just a bit depressing mostly because it was getting dark and I still had a long way to go. I sprinted into Kendal and by the time I got to Windermere Youth Hostel in the Lake District it was night.

The next day cycling north through the Lake District came as a bit of a shock as I was in the mountains but it was an easy ride as the roads I took ran along the valley floor. It was hot that afternoon as I crossed the bridge over the South Tyne River. I spotted people paddling in the river so I turned my cycle down to the water and joined in the paddling. The next day I cycled along the famous old Roman wall, Hadrian's Wall, checking out mile forts and museums and ended up at the Youth Hostel in a forest at Bellingham.

Next morning and I was cycling to Scotland. I started the day at a local café having an English Breakfast of eggs, bacon, fried tomatoes, fried mushrooms, fried bread and baked beans with toast and a strong mug of tea. Breakfast done I cycled up to the Scottish border where I stopped to mark the occasion when a carpet delivery truck pulled up.
'Where are you off to,' said a short man with a cockney accent. 'I'm going to Kirkcaldy then on to Dundee, want a lift?'
'Okay,' I said.
He took me to meet his boss in Kirkcaldy who lived in a very Australian looking brand new suburb in a very Australian looking brand new bungalow. I satg down on a very Australian looking lounge suit,

sandwiches arrived made with sliced supermarket bread. I felt like I'd never left Australia until the family started to talk, they were speaking English but their Scottish accent was so thick that I couldn't understand a word.

The carpet delivery fella dropped me in Dundee and the town was full of life. I cycled down to a B&B on the waterfront, checked in and then went back to the town centre to get something to eat and it was as if a nuclear bomb had been dropped on the place, there wasn't a soul to be seen. The town centre was utterly dead and I went to bed hungry. Next morning I got stuck into another full English Breakfast at the B&B. I was joking with the Scottish road workers staying there, they left and the owner, an old lady in her eighties, kept bringing me and two English guests more and more toast and more and more tea and coffee. I can say here that I had a very leisurely morning. Just before I left the old lady took me aside and asked me did I know her best friend who had immigrated to Queensland in Australia fifty years before. Australia at that stage had a population somewhere around twenty million people so I was polite but told her no I didn't.

Before I cycled off to Pitlochry, my next stop, I dropped into a corner shop to buy something for lunch. The old lady behind the counter ask me where I was from, 'Australia,' I said then she launched into a long speech about an Australian television show called The Sullivans and asked me what was going to happen in the up and coming episodes. I told her I didn't watch television and she said: 'Don't watch television must be reading too many dirty books.' I laughed.

I cycled up to a great hydro dam it was Pitlochry. There was a Youth Hostel, a distillery and a repertory theatre in the town so I stayed three days and saw all the plays on the repertoire. One day I cycled out to Ben Vrackie the local Mountain at 2759 feet above sea level. I cycled in docksider shoes as they were very versatile and in that ultra-light footwear, wearing shorts and a T shirt, I zipped up the mountain passing many Scottish mountaineers as they struggled up in big heavy boots with big heavy packs on their backs. I got to the top and there was a concrete cairn and a fantastic view then I skipped down again passing all the Scottish mountaineers still on their way up.

At the Youth Hostel in Pitlochry I met two nice girls from Glasgow and they told me all the ins and outs of cooking Scotland's most famous dish, haggis. So the next day I bought a haggis from the local butcher, neaps and tatties, that's turnips and potatoes and cooked up a big dinner. When it was all cooked I served it up and sprinkled on salt and pepper as is the custom and we got stuck in. The girls asked me what I thought. 'Yes good,' I said. It pays to be polite. Talking of Scottish food at one Youth Hostel I found a packet of porridge that had been left for others to eat so I cooked it up and it was the best porridge I've ever eaten.

From Pitlochry I cycled north up a long valley with mountains on either side, no houses, no shops, no trees, it reminded me of the vast barren open country of Australia. I got to a very small town, possibly Dalwhinnie, and then turned south east, I was making for Fort William. When you visit Scotland it rains all the time, that's the theory anyway, on this trip it rained only once and that was a light drizzle. I cycled past great hydro dams and as it hadn't rained they were completely devoid of water. The bottom of the dams were just mud with tiny little streams snaking through them.

Other than sleeping I didn't do anything else at Fort William which was a pity as Ben Nevis is there, Scotland's highest mountain, I would have liked to climb it. Instead I cycled off to Stirling Castle and then onto Edinburgh as I was going to the famous Edinburgh Arts Festival. I had tickets for the opera, The Magic Flute, and a play by a Glasgow theatre company about World War One.

The only other interesting event was on my last day I was cycling to the railway station to get a train south when a truck sped past me and my bike and we were almost dragged under the truck by the suction. I held on for dear life and managed not to get squashed by the trucks big wheels. One thing I found interesting was that when I cycled from Ramsgate to Land's End the year before the spokes on my back wheel were forever popping but on this trip I didn't have one spoke break. The country was more mountainous than Cornwall but the roads went along the valleys and there was less pressure on the back wheel than in hilly Cornwall. Cycling in Cornwall and Devon was some of the toughest cycling I've ever done just for the sheer number of hills I had to climb. Still my bike handled them with ease. Scotland I found was easy cycling.

The Way of the Roses

There's a bike trail that crosses England, from Morecombe near Lancashire on the Irish Sea to Settle in the Yorkshire Dales, the trail then moves on to the old Viking town of York with its famous minster and finishes at Bridlington on the North Sea. A lady by the name of Lorna Runs did it with her husband in four days. She wrote in her blog: 'The route…is utterly beautiful all the way. It's incredibly varied from narrow country lanes, flat roads that wound their way through tiny villages with beautiful cottages, undulating roads, steep hills, some lanes with holes and grit and gravel, some that felt briefly 'off road' and went through the middle of a large field. Every bit of it is however, completely doable on a road bike even for me.'

In 2024 Rob Ainsley, from York, cycled it in 1970's fashion. He wrote: 'I'm doing the Way of the Roses 1970s style. On a 1978 bike and using only seventies kit. No gadgets, no lycra. a rain cape not GORE-TEX jacket. Terrible old Ever Ready lights, not LEDs. Fixing accommodation on the hoof, in a callbox or by word of mouth. A 35mm SLR camera taking black and white photographs. Cash only, no credit cards. In short, nothing which was unavailable in 1978. No internet, email, mobile phones, GPS, cleats, Channel 4, real ale, avocados or Banoffee Pie.' What the heck is Banoffee Pie you might say, well it's a combination of a crunchy cracker crust, soft and sweet dulce de leche, thick slices of fresh banana, and a mountain of billowy whipped cream, sounds like heaven to some but not me.

Back to the Coast to Coast, Rob set out from Morecombe and encountered hills for two days and driving rain but what's interesting is the phone boxes. His plan was to use telephone boxes to book B&B accommodation just like in the seventies problem was the few that still exist don't use cash anymore and they are used as a public toilet by the local bird population, some just don't work and one had been turned into a sound art installation.

After four days of cycling: 'I learned that much of what makes bike touring a pleasure is still there. And I found it on my 1970s style Way of the Roses. Quiet lanes, country scenery, village cafes, chatting with fellow travellers, the joy of self-contained travel… these things don't change. Never mind the past; here's to the future.'

The Katy Trail

The Katy Trail is a 240 mile long trail stretching across the state of Missouri in the American Mid-West. On the Katy Trail you can ride beneath towering river bluffs, meander through peaceful farmland and visit small-town Americana. The Katy Trail's name originates from the Missouri-Kansas-Texas (MKT) Railroad, the railroad was commonly referred to as "The Katy" due to its "K-T" stock market symbol.

Erika from Kansas City wrote: 'I started riding about seven to eight years ago. I won my bike through workforce wellness points and while I have made lots of upgrades, my bike is still an entry level hybrid that was originally free! Cycling combines with my late dad's love of the Katy Trail and my need to retire from running, cycling has become my happy place.

'My dad picked up cycling in retirement but was more of a casual day trip rider. His Katy Trail trips were low mileage days staying at B&B's with my mum meeting him along the way by car. Sadly I did not become a cyclist until he was no longer able to ride, but I took his love of being outside on the trails and turned it into my own bikepacking hobby.

'I lost my dad four years ago. I only wish I had discovered this hobby back when he was still healthy and riding the Katy Trail. I wish I could tell him every story today. He would love to hear all about the trails and the community around them, the cyclists who pass through from all over the world and the friends I have made.'

Hell on Earth

I was talking to my brother Colin who has a carbon fibre racing bike and my typical thoughts were that they are not very rugged but Colin tole me that his bike was a carbon fibre racing bike that's very rugged as it's designed to race on cobble stones. It's made in California by an American company Specialised founded in 1974 and the bike's called A Paris-Roubaix Edition. This is a one day professional bicycle road race in northern France starting in Paris and finishing in Roubaix at the border with Belgium.

The race is one of the oldest cycling races, first run in 1896 and is a classic in the European cycling calendar. It's famous for rough terrain and cobblestones and has been called Hell on Earth. The cyclists can end up covered in mud, and punctures and mechanical problems are common but it's not called Hell on Earth because of that. After World War One some journalists travelled north to suss out what damage the trench warfare of the war had done to the bicycle racing course. As they travelled north they discovered that the air reeked of broken drains, raw sewerage and the stench of rotting cattle, trees were blackened stumps and everywhere was mud. The journalist thought that they had been to Hell on Earth.

After World War Two the race was called by an enthusiast: 'The last great madness of cycling'. Efforts had to be made to preserve the cobblestone roads which were rapidly being resurfaced and there are still cobblestones but not like there once was. A representative of Mavic, a company providing support for the various bicycle racing teams wrote: 'Every year we change fewer wheels, because the wheels and tyres are getting better and better. We changed about 20 wheels today. Five years ago, it was much worse we'd be changing about a hundred.' Quite some race really.

My brother described his bike: 'It's a very smooth ride built to race on rough roads with a super light and stiff frame with a tapered head tube to give internal suspension. All the cables are inside the frame and the gears are controlled by moving the brake levels. The same design that the professional riders use in the Paris to Roubaix Race'

Part Nine
Collecting

The Weird and the Wonderful

Bicycle collecting, especially antique pieces and the English club bikes of the second half of the 20th century, has become a pastime across the world. Around 2022 Tony Stuart who lives in Melbourne Australia found his father-in-law's 1976 Raleigh which as a project he did up for his son to ride. After about two years his son stopped using the Raleigh so Tony took it one day down to the shops, he enjoyed the ride so much that he started ridding the old bike. At the time he owned a classic car which cost a fortune to keep on the road and he hardly ever got it on to the road he spent a fortune trying to keep it on. So he sold his classic car and started collecting bikes. What makes a person a collector, hard to say really but there you go.

Tony was a designer come architect so he was interested in bikes with novel designs. In his collection he has a Pedersen bike designed in Denmark, A Moulton, the first of the small wheel bikes and a penny farthing, the bikes with the big front wheel and the small back wheel. Now Tony has moved on to collecting English club bikes of the 1960's to the 1980's and his shed is crammed with 32 bikes plus more in his workshop. The bikes aren't there just to look pretty however he has a loop circuit around his house of 2-3 kilometres and he takes up to three bikes out for a run every day.

I asked him which bike he loved best and he replied that he loves them all but one of his favourites is a 1949 Raleigh Record Ace perhaps the only one in Australia. Tony said that he really enjoys riding it and it makes him feel good when he does. The Raleigh catalogue stated: 'A product embodying the combined experience and advice of club and track men, in collaboration with the 'quality conscious' technicians of the Raleigh organisation, whose unequalled skill and craftsmanship have produced a mount incorporating all the needs of the most critical rider. We are satisfied that in the Record Ace we are offering a speedman's mount which is without equal in the industry.'

'My favourite Aussie Bike in my collection,' said Tony, 'is my 1959 Spearman made in Woolongong. It's a racing bike with Zeus derailleurs, Nervex lugs and other high end parts, I bought it in a fairly unloved state. It had a broken chain stay that I had replaced and I spent some time repairing the rather nice paint job where it got burnt during the repair. I decided I wanted a 50s English club bike look so rebuilt the wheels with a Sturmey Archer 3 speed hub and added the red Bluemel mudguards. It rides great, light, nimble and fast. It's like an Australian Record Ace.'

An interesting bike in Tony's collection is the Pedersen: developed by Danish inventor Mikael Pedersen and produced in the English town of Dursley. It's main feature is a hammock style seat and a cantilever frame. To put it quite simply it looks odd with a high frame sticking up at the front. The Pedersen is often described as the most comfortable bike ever but Tony hasn't found it so. He says it seems to be designed for tall people and he can't get the saddle low enough. To get off the bike is a problem he has to jump off while it's still going as the hummock seat is so high.

Tony has a Penny Farthing built in Evandale Tasmania about 25 years ago and he has taken it back to Evandale for the annual Penny Farthing races. He came third or fourth in his first race ever and hopes to do better next time. When he first tried out on a penny farthing he found that instantly he could ride. It was hard to mount so he incorporated a second step to get up on the seat above the big fifty two inch wheel. I asked him how fast he could go and he said that he had done thirty two kilometres an hour but sitting on a penny farthing you are right in the wind. In Evandale, where they rode into a forty kilometre wind, they peddled like mad just to go at four kilometres an hour.

Tony has three Moultons in his collections. Dr Alex Moulton helped with the design for the wheels and the suspension of the famous Morris Mini Minor motor car and he took his expertise in small wheels and suspension to the development of the Moulton bicycle with its small wheels and front and back suspension both revolutionary ideas for the time.

When I asked Tony about the performance of the Moulton he said they are slightly overrated, it's speedy but not that lightweight and after twenty kilometres he gets an ache in his shoulders. He said was that he had to get used to riding a bike with small wheels, possibly swapping between a big wheeled bike and a small wheeled bike is not so good.

With his shed full of bikes and no room left, he is at the stage that when he gets a new bike an old one has to go. He plans to bring his present collection up to scratch working on the paint job on the frames and he is busy rebuilding Bell Saddles. Bell saddles were a Sydney based company from the 50's and 60's and often have a kangaroo imprinted on the leather of the saddle. To repair saddles Tony builds a template first and every saddle needs a new template I guess it will keep him busy for a while yet. I wish Tony happy collecting and happy riding.

Part Ten
Short & Sweet

In the Bag

An old gentleman here in Ross who owns a fold up bike told me about the time he cycled down to the ferry at the Attersee, a lake in upper Austria twenty kilometres long and four kilometres wide. He paid his fair but the ticket collector insisted that he pay for the bike as well. The old gentleman said;
'Is my baggage free?'
'Yes,' said the ticket collector.
So the old gentleman sat down with his fold up bike, folded it up put it in its bicycle carry bag and walked onto the ferry.

Talking about bicycle bags, I love Carradice cycle bags especially the ones made from cotton duct ,they just look absolutely stylish. Carradice started producing bike bags in 1932 when Wilf Carradice couldn't find a bike bag he liked for his bicycle touring adventures so he made his own. In those days bike bags were made from either leather or rubber and Wilf's friends all ordered the cotton bags so the business in Nelson Lancashire was born. Not only was it born but it is still going! Carradice make the most beautiful selection of saddle bags and panniers. A bag made from cotton duct, called the Barley Saddle Bag, is very retro and reminds me of an old fashioned Norwegian back pack. A gentleman by the name of Ke Vin wrote on Facebook: 'I carried a 15 foot Turkish carpet once in my Carradice saddle bag.' I could imagine an enormous carpet hanging off the back of a bike!

In the Drink
Grant, the postman here in Ross, was born in England. His family migrated to Australia and then shut up shop and went home again, then they grew tired of England and found themselves Down Under once more. While at school in England Grant and his brother had beautiful Raleigh bikes. Grant and his brother, being Australian, were more self-confident than the local lads and were dating girls two years older than themselves the local lads didn't like that. One day Grant and his brother were fishing down at the canal and the local lads turned up and threatened to beat them up. Grant told them it wouldn't be a good idea to do that as his dad would belt shit out of them.
'Which bikes are yours?' one of the local lads said.
Grant pointed to a couple of bikes which the local boys picked up and threw into the canal. Grant and

his brother then jumped up, ran to their own bikes and sped away as fast as they could peddle. The bikes in the drink belonged to someone else.

In the Flesh

My friend Ros told me of the time she was cycling in Ireland. 'My girlfriend and I went on a bicycle holiday to Ireland. This was about 1982. We pulled up at a lovely typically Irish pub and asked for directions to the nearest town where we might get some repairs done to my friend's bike. Alternatives given were the short way, involving a serious climb that we were assured was all downhill from the top and had the best view of Wicklow, or the long way which involved such things as left at the blue house, second left after the shrine to Bridig and twists and turns guaranteed to get us lost or sold to white slavers. So we tackled the hill. The sun came out. We rested at a farm and my chum went behind a haystack to swap her long trousers for shorts. There was a shriek and she came running chased by a man with a pitchfork.

In the Wind

Holland is often touted as a great place to cycle as it's flat and has lots of cycle paths but it's not always that simple as my friend Andrea wrote: 'I remember cycling in Holland. You'd think it would be easy cos it's flat but the wind would blow and blow. Damn awful if it was a head wind or a cross wind. Which it is seventy five percent of the time.'

There is a Tide in the Affairs of Men
My friend David had a Malvern Star Five Star bike. He said it was pretty specky in those days, late sixties, and he used to go to Brown Hill Creek in the Adelaide Hills and charge about speeding down hill and over the bumps. Problem was that this was the time before mountain bikes and bikes weren't made to withstand that level of punishment and one day the frame of his bike just split apart.

As he told me the tale I imagined David landing on his face in a mud puddle being air lifted to hospital by helicopter and taking three years of rehabilitation for him walk again. The truth was, as David put it, 'Metal fatigue occurred on the diagonal tubing close to the headset. I didn't come off in a spectacular accident the thing snapped just as I was finishing my ride.'

On another occasion David and his girlfriend cycled off up the coast north of Adelaide, found a nice spot on the beach to pitch their tent and bunkered down for the night. Problem this time was that the tide came in and in the middle of the night they were inundated by the sea. Then they were racing around trying to gather up their kit, their bikes and a pair of contact lenses that went missing.

A Hero of our Time

Alistair Wyper, another keen cyclist, wrote on facebook: 'I've been a Phil Anderson fan for a long while and one day in 2007 I met my hero. I was cycling up the Col du Soulor (a mountain pass in France) to see the Tour de France finish when I was overtaken at speed by a cyclist. I thought that looks like Phil Anderson, he was leading a group of cyclists wearing Aussie jerseys. I caught up with them and spoke with the tailender. He confirmed that it was the great man himself leading a tour group. I came up with him and told him he was a hero of mine having ridden thirteen tour de Frances. He was very friendly and said: I was a hero for cycling up the Col with panniers. My kit was packed away in a pair of Carradice panniers on the front of my bike.'

Phil Anderson is a British born Australian former racing cyclist who was the first non-European to wear the yellow jersey in the Tour de France. If you win a section of the tour you get to wear the yellow jersey, the symbol of the Tour.

Boots an All
David Carmen, from Rotorua New Zealand, runs Soigneur, Merino Cycling Jerseys. The word Soigneur if you are wondering means cycle racing back up crew. Anyway David an ex-racing cyclist makes cycling jerseys from merino wool. His bespoke cycling jerseys are now worn all over the world. You can pick your own style, colours and logo, how brilliant is that? To top it off you get a brilliant natural fibre instead of factory made synthetic rubbish.

Another great cycling product are the cycling shoes made in Derbyshire England in a town called Stoney Middleton. In 1897 William Lennon stated making boots for miners and quarry workers, the business expanded but in the 1950's all the old machinery for hand making boots was put into storage, times had changed and work boots were made differently. Then early this century the old machines were hauled out, refurbished and William Lennon and Co started to make traditional leather boots, they even make old army boots and lovely soft leather cycling shoes.

Freedom

Suzanne Buxton a very keen cyclist from Yorkshire wrote: 'When I was young my dad brought home a Raleigh Twenty with 20 inch wheels. He told me that it was a racing bike and would be for me. The paintwork was all scratched so he painted it dark blue with some paint he had in his workshop. I was allowed to watch him build it and pass him tools, which made me feel very important. My dad was a mechanic by trade and before this I was hardly ever allowed in his workshop and not allowed to touch his tools at all. It was all very exciting.

In a few weeks the bike was ready. Me and my dad went on a cycling adventure down a nearby lane. He taught me how to ride by saying if I pedalled he would hold on to my seat at the back. He didn't hold onto my seat, it didn't matter. I was already faster than him when we raced. Or so he let me think.

A couple of days later I was on my bike and decided to go on an adventure. Down a nearby lane there were some horses so I rode to see them. It felt like miles, but was probably only a few hundred yards. The next day I repeated my journey, but took carrots from the kitchen for the horses. I repeated this several times over the next week sometimes taking carrots, sometimes apples. Then my dad noticed things were disappearing from the vegetable cupboard. I was grounded! The sense of freedom and adventure that bike gave me was well worth being grounded.

Part Eleven
Cycling Down Under

The Bay of Fires on a Linus Gaston 3

Many years later, I'm a cyclist once more and with my Gaston 3 I was desperate to hit the Tasmanian roads. Tasmania, off the south coast of mainland Australia, is a great place for bicycle touring and the east coast of Tasmania makes for a great bike ride. This little tour is at the top of the east coast, a place called the Bay of Fires said to be the most beautiful beach in the world.

Actually we started this ride not in the Bay of Fires but slightly inland where the St Helens Point road meets the Tasman Highway. Here is a pedestrian bicycle track that swings around the shore of Georges Bay with a view of the fishing village of St Helens, of farmland and the distant mountains. It's a lovely ride next to the sea. Eventually we came to a bridge and we were in St Helens. There is a floating fish and chip restaurant in the harbour, what more could you want? And there are some lovely fishing boats moored there. We cycled along the front, Sue on her mixte, she calls it Rosie and me on my

Gaston 3, I call it Caff after Café Racer. St Helens is on a tidal inlet chock-a-block with bird life and we cruised along until we came to the main road to Binalong Bay.

There is a sort of bike path come footpath that weaves along the shore, it crosses the road from time to time but even though it's a very informal bike track it's a joy to ride. As we turned onto the track the path crossed a causeway through swampy dairy pastures and in the distance, as always in Tasmania, were mountains. We cycled around the bay enjoying ourselves thoroughly and then the track ran out. The problem with no track in Tasmania is that although the roads are bitumen and very good, they are often very narrow and even though motorists give you a wide berth the four wheel drivers always seem to be driving as if they are taking a dying relative to hospital.

There is an oyster farm on the left where fresh oyster are available and they are delicious and cheap. Then we were cycling in the bush, Tasmanian blue gums towered above and wattles and heath, banksias and lots more filled in the undergrowth. Slowly we made our way up hill to have the absolute joy of freewheeling down but then we were sorry that we had enjoyed ourselves so much as there was another hill to climb and this one was longer and steeper and involved a bit of pushing. All was worthwhile however as there before us was Grants Lagoon and Binalong Bay, quite spectacular. We charged down to the beach with its little boat harbour and the lookout over the granite rocks. There are lots of granite rocks covered in orange lichen, quite appropriate for a bay that sweeps around the north east coast of Tasmania and is called the Bay of Fires.

We now cycled back to the turnoff that took us to The Gardens eleven kilometres down the road. The road, although a good one, is hilly. It starts with a nice stampede downhill only to be followed by a slow climb up the other side. Oh well what goes around comes around. We cycled through forest and there were wallabies and small kangaroos, who hopped away as we cycled by. There is free camping at several spots along this bit of coast so you can bring your bike and your tent and hang out. We cycled up into hilly country again with more great beaches off to the side, Swimcart Beach, Cosy Corner and Sloop Reef. Sloop Reef is a mass of granite jutting out into the sea, off Sloop Reef is

Pinnacle Rock, that's what I call it anyway, and a sea eagle landed atop as we watched.

After this little detour we cycled back to the bitumen and found ourselves on a hilltop, we hurtled down the hill and came to the best bit of the ride, on our left were lagoons and on our right the crashing waves of the aqua sea. We crossed a bridge, explored Taylors Beach briefly and then rode by Sloop Lagoon which was full of black swans. The cycling was fairly easy apart from the wind and the road was straight and safe and a joy to cruise along. After the lagoon is coastal heath, all very beautiful and more Pacific Ocean. At the end of this section of road is a parking bay that gets you onto the northern end of Taylors Beach at Honeymoon Point. It's incredible there, the waves crash in brilliant white froth against the majestic blue all along the length of golden sand and on the rocks the spray smashes up into the air sending tiny rainbows into the sky.

We stirred ourselves and headed back to the bitumen, crossed the lagoon on a narrow bridge, we were up hilling it now, but soon emerged onto a windy, heathy, grassland with cattle roaming the fields. There were great views and the little road passed a few holiday shacks and then before us was the trig point and the lookout at The Gardens. The Gardens were named thus because of the plethora of native flowers that bloom there in spring.

We walked up the track to the lookout, the view takes in the whole of the Bay of Fires, we could see Binalong Bay to the south and Policeman's Point and Eddystone Lighthouse to the north. There is a long silver golden strand of sand, the aqua sea and beautiful bright orange granite rocks and the whole place has a certain magical atmosphere that is a rare thing to find and hard to describe, it is a magical place.

Speed Five
The tyres on my Linus Café Racer suddenly wore out so I ordered new ones. Would you believe it, I read the size from the tyre wall of my bike and when the new tyres arrived they were far too big! I reordered but in the meantime I had no bike. For some reason I started looking at the Pashley Classic Bikes on their web site and before I knew it I, with Sue's encouragement, had ordered a Pashley Speed Five. The truth is I'd always wanted one.

The Speed Five was flown over to Australia from Stratford-upon-Avon and delivery took just over a week. My new bike had a Reynolds 531 frame, was hand made with lugs, Sturmey Archer FIVE yes Five speed gears, Sturmey Archer hub brakes, a Brooks leather racing saddle, semi dropped handlebars like old fashioned racing bikes, and no mudguards or any non-essential fittings. It's a 1920's style Path Racer and looks magic. While waiting for it I rode Sue's girl's bike, a Linus mixte and came back with legs of jelly. I said to Sue: 'That bike's terrible, (I don't like girls bikes), you should try my old one.' She got on my old Linus boy's bike, she'd never ridden a boy's bike before and she loved it. 'It must have an electric motor somewhere as it goes so fast,' she said.

When my new bike was delivered I rode it around the town, it's a brilliant machine and I love it. It's bigger and heavier than I would have thought but it goes like a dream. It makes my old Linus Café Racer look like a kids' bike. It's fast and powerful and here in Tasmania, where we have to face the Roaring Forties most days, it feels like it eats the wind. 'Can I try your new bike?' said Sue. 'Yes of course,' I said. She got on, circled around the car park by the famous Ross Bridge. 'You're cheating,' she said. What she meant was that it was so fast and powerful that it made my Linus Café Racer that she was now riding look like a pigmy. 'I know I can't have one but I want one,' was her next comment.

We bought Sue a Pashley Gov'nor GT, a 1920's style Path Racer but this one has eight internal hub gears, hub breaks, a hub dynamo and is a beautiful Secret Blue with white tyres. My Speed Five is racing car green by the way. To cap it off we also bought Books leather saddle bags and for long trips we bought Carradice saddle bags, handmade in Lancashire England. Sue's bike is a beautiful thing and retro as well.

So the point is, where possible, try out a bike before you buy. Sue said my Linus Café Racer always looked too small for me and Sue's mixte, we knew, was too small for her. My Linus Café Racer is technically the same size as the Pashley Speed Five but they are worlds apart. One size does not fit all! The end result of my tyres wearing thin is that Sue and I are broke but we have two new bikes that we love to ride.

Guv'nor

Sue got a Pashley Guv'nor GT and I asked Dave who handles international sales at Pashley why it was called a Guv'nor. 'It was called the Guv'nor because Adrian, the Managing Director, had the design idea of the bike he personally wanted to ride. So it was made for him and it took off from there. So it was as you say named after the Guv'nor.'

Adrian, the managing director, wrote of the Guv'nor: 'Whilst I admire all of Pashley's bicycles, the Guv'nor will always be 'my true love'. Inspired by our original 'Path Racer', I first conceived it in 2007 as my cycle to work bike. Little did I know then that it would capture the imagination of riders around the world! I still ride the very first production model, complete with its double top tube and custom burr walnut mudguards—a timeless classic that continues to stir the heart.'

The Guv'nor is certainly a good looking and very photogenic bike with its white tyres, Brooks leather saddle, North Road handlebars and black body work.

The Oatlands Rail Trail

The Oatlands Rail Trail in central Tasmania is more a walking trail come bike path, it's eight kilometres one way and a fairly easy ride. Sue and I did this trail so Sue could get used to riding her Guv'nor on off road bike tracks before going on to bigger and better things. It's a nice little ride.

We had never carried bikes on our Renault Clio, it's a small car and the bikes are almost bigger than the car! The bike rack arrived by post and we had fun and games fitting it, to be honest it didn't look very strong. Then on the Friday the wind had dropped, we live in Tasmania right in the path of the Roaring Forties and the wind is constant, so light winds meant we had to go. We loaded our bikes, the Pashley Speed Five and the Pashley Guv'nor GT, so far so good. We drove to the Ross post office, we had a parcel in the post. We inspected the load, all good. I picked up the parcel. Tentatively we drove the forty kilometres to Oatlands and happily the bikes were totally stable on the rack.

In Oatlands, next to Lake Dulverton with its coots and black Swans and in view of the Callington Mill, a traditional Dutch type windmill, we unloaded the bikes. The carrier had come up trumps the bikes and the car hadn't been damaged, all was well. I opened my package it was a handmade Carradice Junior Saddle Bag. It was a beauty made by a lady named

Sue and it fitted my bike like a glove, well actually like a saddle bag. We put a camera, gloves and a tool kit in it then we were off.

The track was made up of rather rough gravel and there were no cars about so we cruised the road alongside the lake. Then the track improved and we started to cycle on the trail next to the lake. We trundled along came to an old settlers cottage, the ruins of an old World War Two flax mill and an aboriginal heritage site with shallow sandstone caves all worth a Captain Cook, that's a look in Australiana and after a short break we were off again.

Then we were cycling on the old railway but not for long. The track left the railway and twisted and turned around the lake. When I write lake, at its deepest it's only three meters and in a dry year it can almost completely dry up. Its saving glory however are the black swans, at times there are hundreds of them. We came to a bend and passed a pile of rusting discarded night soil buckets, the fields near there had been the night soil depository for the town and once grew abundant crops of potatoes.

Oatlands was now in the distance and we were cycling down to the main road to Parattah. The trail turned into a rough cycle walking trail beside the road. We passed lovely banksias and eucalyptus trees and a native forest of white gums. Often we came around blind corners only to be confronted by a hump that we weren't ready for, the trick was to cycle in a slightly lower gear to be ready for the unexpected. Then the trail seemed to run out. We were hedged in between the road and a barbed wire fence, with litter scattered here and there, not our preferred option. We pushed on, Parattah appeared and soon we pulled into the old station. There was a picnic ground with picnic tables but we hadn't brought a picnic.

Going back to Oatlands was easy peasy, it was downhill freewheeling all the way. Back in Oatlands we cycled to the supermarket and bought a few essentials and christened the Carradice bag and then roamed the back streets. Oatlands like Ross, where we live, is a heritage town with beautiful old sandstone buildings dating back to the settlement of Tasmania so a cruise through the streets on one's trusty deadly treadly is well worth the effort. All in all a successful first trip.

The Scottsdale Rail Trail

We told the owner of the self-contained cabin where we were staying that we were going to do the Scottsdale Rail Trail and he embarked on a long story of how he and his wife when they first came to the area had ridden the rail trail and his wife had come off her bike and the guard on the chain of her bike had cut a deep wound into her leg, she had taken months to recover and still bore the scar. We didn't need to know that!

The fifty two kilometre return ride in north east Tasmania started on a good bit of Asphalt at the Scottsdale railway station but it didn't last. Soon we were on what I would call rough gravel and we bumped along with machine gunned regularity. First off we had to avoid the dog walkers as we rolled down hill through lush farming country. It was a strange feeling being on one's bike, my Pashley Speed Five and not needing to peddle. My bike just rolled on, the only drawback was the constant little stones, bump bump bump.

We came to the main highway dismounted and crossed it, we were to do this again later. Now we were cycling on the flat through a semi-industrial district. We stopped. 'How you doing?' I asked Sue.

'I'm fine,' she said. Sue had never been on a long bike ride before and had never ridden over a rough gravel track so I was concerned but as she said, she was fine. After we crossed the road for a second time we were in lush green farming country again then we came to Tonganah where there was a toilet so we had a toilet stop. We cycled around a lake got back onto the rail trail and were climbing. It was gentle climbing, I just geared down a bit and I didn't even really notice that I was cycling uphill, very enjoyable apart from the stones. Oh yes and if the stones weren't bad enough there were lots of sheoaks, a tree rather like a pine but not a pine, but like pines they have cones of a sort about the size of large marbles and in places hundreds of sheoak cones covered the track, bump bump bump bump!.

The jewel in the crown of the Scottsdale Rail Trail suddenly appeared. A railway cutting that was lined with what the Tasmanian's call man ferns and the Australian's tree ferns. More and more cuttings would appear along the old rail line and they have now been taken over by these giant ferns. It's like cycling through fairyland or Jurassic Park.

The rail trail snaked around the hills. The snaking was originally engineered so that the trains would have a gentle climb through what was almost rain forest, trains not really being able to climb hills. I saw some beautiful mountain ash, the tallest flowering trees in the world. The bark of the mountain ash comes off in great ribbons and the new bark is quite white, they are beautiful rain forest giants. We cycled on over the gravel, rattle rattle rattle, and suddenly there was a tree down completely blocking the track. We tried to move it but no go. I was about to carry our bikes across the downed tree when suddenly three Victorian's arrived on electric bikes. We discussed the problem and with sheer brute force we pushed the downed tree aside. Those Victorian's were a godsend. Before they left one of the Victorians loved our Pashley bikes so much that he had to have a photo of Sue and me and our bikes.

We let the Victorians go ahead, we like to cycle together just Sue and I. Sue noticed a black stain on the front of my bike, it looked like grease, I flicked it off. It wasn't grease it was a blood sucking leach and it hung onto one of my fingers until I pulled it off. Downed trees and leeches, this ride was turning into an Africa Queen style adventure.

We cycled on, to our side was a sheer tree lined drop down the mountain. In the distance was more lush farming country and on the horizon the sea. We passed through more and more fern lined cuttings and came to the ruin of Trewalla station and noted it down as a place to stop for lunch on our decent. The track started to deteriorate after this as loggers had done a lot of harvesting in the area. The land was clear felled and the track was not smooth. After the brief area of logging we were back in the forest and then finally we came to Billycock Hill and Tulendeena Station. Don't imagine a great all singing and dancing railway station it was just a platform and a shelter shed. This was the end of the line so we turned our bikes around and started to roll down. The rolling down went on for 16 kilometres, it was fun and a strange feeling not to need to pedal. We stopped for a brief snack at Trewalla station and then rolled on. Down down we rolled and the only thing that spoilt it was the endless bump bump bump. We crossed the road cycled through the small semi-industrial section and then cycled up hill to Scottsdale Station. Later as I sat on the side of the road adjusting the bicycle carrier, that fits onto our car, with my Brooks multitool I said, 'Would have been better on a mountain bike.' Sue agreed and said, 'I enjoyed it but I never want to cycle on gravel again'.

The next day we drove to George Town where there is a trail between George Town on the Tamar River and Low Head at the mouth of the river. When we got out of the car to take the bikes off the back the wind wiped up around us, so we quickly put on more clothes. The views across the Tamar Estuary were great but compared to the Scottsdale Rail Trail the track was not as spectacular however it was concrete and it was bliss to cycle on a smooth track. We cycled along easily the wind was behind us. We came to nice beaches and inlets a small park and then the old Pilots Station appeared. It was a series of beautiful old white stone buildings reminiscent of old Cornwall in England. Eventually we came up to the old lighthouse, geared down and pushed up the final slope.

We took photographs of the rugged coastline then turned our bikes into the wind and cycled down and along the track passing beaches, suburbs and avoiding dog walkers. When we got back to the car Sue was buggered. We had been away for three days. The first day we had climbed, on foot, Mount Stonach not a big mountain but at times the almost vertical walking trail had been totally messed up by off road dirt bikes of the motorized variety. The bed rock was granite and had turned to dust. Going up was hard but coming down on granite dust was a nightmare. The view across lush farmland and out to sea from the granite top was beautiful though. The second day was the Scottsdale Rail Trail which apart from the bumping wasn't hard but it was a 52 kilometre ride and day three was the Kalamaluka Trail, George Town to Low Head, that was only 12 kilometres return, the return however was into the wind. Sue was worn out. 'I enjoyed it, it was a pleasure to just ride and not have to watch where you were going all the time,' she said.

We reloaded the bikes on the car, checked them and double checked and then we were off going home to Ross in the Tasmanian Midlands. When we got home we discovered that the bike carrier slung on the back of the car had started to scratch the paintwork on the hatch. We ordered a tow bar and a bigger and a better bike rack to go on it. When the tow bar was fitted and the new bike rack arrived we took off to Devonport to do the first part of what I call The Penguin Rail Trail. From the mouth of the Mersey River to Turners Beach an easy twelve kilometres and back. At Turners Beach we had lunch at a lookout over the coast, the sun was shining and as it was winter we felt warm and good. In the spring we planned to do the whole coastal track.

The Blue Mountains Rail Trail
In 2026 Sue and I are planning to do three rail trails in Victoria and a shorter one in New South Wales. We are going to start with the Yarra Valley Rail Trail at Lilydale just outside Melbourne, a beautiful trail with a good surface in the Dandenong Ranges. Then we go north to Bright under Mt Buffalo and cycle the Murray to Mountains Rail Trail it has beautiful scenery and a paved track. We move north again and camp out at Lake Hume and cycle the first part of the High Country Rail Trail along the side of the lake. Finally there is a short trail at Tumbarumba in NSW high country.

The Yarra Valley Rail Trail.
My brother Colin told me of the time he was cycling in Victoria. 'I have done a few rides around Victoria I rode the Yarra Valley Rail Trail in winter, Yes I know, it was a very cold ride, we rode up the hill that wasn't so bad but coming done was freezing. I remember as you cycle along the upper reaches of the Yarra Valley being engulfed by the sounds of running water and the fragrance of nature. We were

surrounded by mountain ash, the tallest flowering tree in the world, they were magnificent.'

The Wine Connoisseurs Rail Trail

I've found a mob of really well surfaced and very scenic rail trails in the wine regions around Adelaide where I went to school and university. We hope to do these in 2026 as well. There is the Barossa Rail Trail, through the Barossa Valley wine region, there's plenty of wine made in the Barossa especially reds. Coast to Vines, another rail trail through the McLaren Vale wine region, this region is also good for red wine. The Amy Gillett Rail Trail in the Adelaide Hills, it's lovely up there and they even make wine of the white variety. They like to call their wine cold climate, in South Australia there is really no such thing as cold climate. Then there is the Encounter Coast Rail Trail along the coast south of Adelaide, they make the odd bottle of plonk, and there's a good rail trail way down south in the Coonawarra a premium South Australian wine region famous for its shiraz. Not to forget the Riesling Trail in the Clare Valley famous for its riesling. Sue and I cycled there when we lived nearby and the best bit is the trail going north of Seven Hills. Seven Hills Cellars created by

Lutheran monks is worth a visit, I've drunk a few bottles of Seven Hills.

Get on your bike and ride!

Other works by Anthony E Thorogood

Jack Hamma Action Adventures

Shakespeare on the Roof
In Bed with Jane Austen
Picnic with Picasso
Miss Marple Struts Her Stuff
Hi Jack
Poirot Packs a Punch
Blind Man's Bluff
Licensed to Thrill
Unconditional Surrender
The Ten Musketeers
The Purple Pimpernel
The Girl with the Golden Gun

Printed in Dunstable, United Kingdom